YOUTH AND HIGHER EDUCATION IN AFRICA

THE CASES OF CAMEROON, SOUTH AFRICA, ERITREA AND ZIMBABWE

YOUTH AND HIGHER EDUCATION IN AFRICA

THE CASES OF CAMEROON, SOUTH AFRICA, ERITREA AND ZIMBABWE

Edited by

Donald P. Chimanikire

Council for the Development of Social Science Research in Africa

© **CODESRIA 2009**
Council for the Development of Social Science Research in Africa
Avenue Cheikh Anta Diop, Angle Canal IV
P.O. Box 3304 Dakar, 18524, Senegal
Website: www.codesria.org

ISBN: 978-2-86978-239-6

All rights reserved. No part of this publication may be reproduced or transmitted in any form or by any means, electronic or mechanical, including photocopy, recording or any information storage or retrieval system without prior permission from CODESRIA.

> Typesetter: Daouda Thiam
> Cover Designer: Ibrahima Fofana
> Printed by Imprimerie Graphi plus, Dakar, Senegal
>
> Distributed in Africa by CODESRIA
> Distributed elsewhere by African Books Collective, Oxford, UK.
> Website: www.africanbookscollective.com

The Council for the Development of Social Science Research in Africa (CODESRIA) is an independent organisation whose principal objectives are to facilitate research, promote research-based publishing and create multiple forums geared towards the exchange of views and information among African researchers. All these are aimed at reducing the fragmentation of research in the continent through the creation of thematic research networks that cut across linguistic and regional boundaries.

CODESRIA publishes a quarterly journal, *Africa Development*, the longest standing Africa-based social science journal; *Afrika Zamani*, a journal of history; the *African Sociological Review*; the *African Journal of International Affairs*; *Africa Review of Books* and the *Journal of Higher Education in Africa*. The Council also co-publishes the *Africa Media Review*; *Identity, Culture and Politics: An Afro-Asian Dialogue*; *The African Anthropologist* and the *Afro-Arab Selections for Social Sciences*. The results of its research and other activities are also disseminated through its Working Paper Series, Green Book Series, Monograph Series, Book Series, Policy Briefs and the CODESRIA Bulletin. Select CODESRIA publications are also accessible online at www.codesria.org.

CODESRIA would like to express its gratitude to the Swedish International Development Cooperation Agency (SIDA/SAREC), the International Development Research Centre (IDRC), the Ford Foundation, the MacArthur Foundation, the Carnegie Corporation, the Norwegian Agency for Development Cooperation (NORAD), the Danish Agency for International Development (DANIDA), the French Ministry of Cooperation, the United Nations Development Programme (UNDP), the Netherlands Ministry of Foreign Affairs, the Rockefeller Foundation, FINIDA, the Canadian International Development Agency (CIDA), IIEP/ADEA, OECD, IFS, OXFAM America, UN/UNICEF, the African Capacity Building Foundation (ACBF) and the Government of Senegal for supporting its research, training and publication programmes.

Table of Contents

Notes on Contributors vii

Introduction
    Donald P. Chimanikire 1

Part 1. Cameroon

Student Activism, Violence and the Politics of Higher
Education in Cameroon: A Case Study of
the University of Buea (1993-2003)
    Jude Fokwang 9

Part 2. South Africa

Post-Apartheid Higher Education: The Role and
Challenges Facing Student Activists
    Mlungisi Cele 35

Part 3. Zimbabwe

Higher Education and Student Politics in Zimbabwe
    Annie Barbra Chikwanha 79

Part 4. Eritrea

Post-war Politics and Higher Education Students in Eritrea
    Berhane Berhe Araia 109

Conclusion
    Donald P. Chimanikire 137

Notes on Contributors

Donald P. Chimanikire holds a PhD in International Studies from Jawarhalal Nehru University, New Delhi. He is former Director of the Institute of Development Studies, University of Zimbabwe and former Chairperson, Department of International Relations and Social Department Studies at the University of Zimbabwe. He is currently a member of the Executive Committee of the Organization for Social Science Research in Eastern and Southern Africa (OSSREA), based in Addis Ababa, Ethiopia.

Annie Barbara Chikwanha holds a PhD in Public Administration from the University of Bergen, Norway. A former lecturer at the Department of Political Science and Administrative Studies, University of Zimbabwe; she is currently a Senior Research Fellow with the Institute for Security Studies in the Nairobi office. She currently heads the Africa Human Security Initiative which has been reviewing crime and criminal justice systems in select Africa Peer Review Member countries. Previously, she worked as a key researcher coordinating nine of the eighteen Afro-Barometer countries that conduct public opinion surveys on democracy and governance. She has written a book chapter on 'Professionalising the Nursing Profession in Zimbabwe', which was published by Copenhagen Business School Press in 2004. She also won the 2006 Elizabeth Nelson Award for the best piece from a country in transition on her book chapter on opinion surveys – Institutional Trust in sub-Saharan Africa'.

Berhane Berhe Araia holds a PhD in Sociology from University of North Carolina, Chapel Hill, USA. He has worked as a lecturer in the Department of Sociology, Social Work and Anthropology, University of Asmara. His research interests are in civil society and democratization in Africa political economy of development, ethnicity and nationalism, war and youth.

Jude Fokwang holds a PhD in Anthropology and is currently a lecturer with the Department of Social Anthropology at the University of Cape Town. In 2006, he was a visiting lecturer in the Department of Anthropology, Rhodes University. His research interests include citizenship, popular culture, democratisation in Africa and postcolonial identities.

Mlungisi Cele is pursuing his doctorate in Education at the University of Western Cape, South Africa. He is currently a director for strategy and planning at the Department of Science and Technology.

Introduction

Donald P. Chimanikire

Background

This network consisted of four young scholars, formerly fellows of the Social Science Research Council who conducted extensive research in the domain of youth, student activism and higher education in Africa. Faithful to this commitment, members of the group intended to advance or buttress various aspects of their study aimed at emphasising the comparative aspects of their different interests. All the members were trained in the social sciences, hence they were endowed with the necessary conceptual and methodological tools to engage in productive and intensive fieldwork that definitely yielded worthy results.

Common to their interests was the theme of youth activism or student politics in institutions of higher education. This was especially true of the post-1990 decade, which was perceived to be the era that marked Africa's 'second independence'. In the cases of Zimbabwe and South Africa, for example, the pillars of apartheid were demolished, giving way to the new democratic dispensation wherein institutions of higher learning were also de-radicalised (de-racialised). Eritrea did not only get its independence in the same decade as South Africa, but issues surrounding student politics became even more controversial. The Eritrean government, for example, imposed national service on their young citizens as a mechanism for involving young people in the nation-building project. However, students became more and more resentful of national service, which led to brutal confrontation with state authorities. In recent years, many African states have tried to assume the right to appoint senior university officials. They have adopted measures which impinge on academic freedom and this has not gone down well with university students. Furthermore, African states have attempted to stifle free speech on campuses and have ignored welfare issues affecting students. The case studies provide a good example of what is happening in many African universities. Hence, this study gives us the results of the trends, nature and operation of student activism in four African countries: Cameroon, Eritrea, South Africa and Zimbabwe.

With regard to student activism *per se*, several theoretical orientations informed the researchers' understanding of the situations in their respective countries. Their research suggest that it went a long way to challenging, modifying or validating prevailing assumptions on student activism in contemporary Africa. One of these approaches maintains that the politics of self-interest enables students to challenge the state when their interests are directly threatened and support it when it suits them. The case studies suggest that students often tend to portray themselves as demoralised individuals who are unlikely to see themselves as bearers of civil and political powers with the identity and status of full citizenship. Hence the tendency to view themselves as victims of an unjust system. It may be that students have a liberalising effect granting that the absence of parental control gives students a chance to undertake various forms of social experimentation with their personal and social identities. This raises the question whether student activism is simply an identity-pursuing project by the youth?

Scholars of youth movements have noted the similarities in expressive style, in romanticism, in idealism, in commitment to violent actions, which have occurred among groups which have varied considerably in their social and political values. Another factor which facilitates student political movement is the physical situation of the university which makes it relatively easy to mobilize students who are disposed to act politically. The campus is the ideal setting where large numbers of people in a common situation can be found.

In the cases of Cameroon, Eritrea, South Africa and Zimbabwe, the study clearly demonstrates that there are four basic issues which underlie the dramatic and often spectacular confrontation between students and the state which came to dominate university politics in the four countries. Essentially, these hinged on efforts by states to encroach on the jealously guarded freedom enjoyed by universities.

The economic decline has also put an end to the anti-imperialist and anti-capitalist alliance between African states and students and other intellectual groupings in the four countries. The 'solidarity' which used to govern the relationship between students and government seems to have ended with the advent of structural adjustment programmes adopted by African governments. In some of the countries studied, the state's ostensible socialist policies have not delivered the goods. Other subjective weaknesses, like corruption, nepotism and regionalism, have become prevalent. The failure of some governments' political and economic policies have led to a rise in frustration and militancy amongst students who are increasingly beginning to feel the pinch.

It is no wonder, therefore, that the case studies of Cameroon, Eritrea, South Africa and Zimbabwe cite some clashes between students and the police over students' demand for an increase in their financial support. Typically, the governments' response in many cases hasbeen slow, and when it came, it was rejected by students as inadequate and not in keeping with the escalating cost of living.

It is also true that one sees a sharp increase in student activism whenever events call accepted political and social values into question, particularly when policy failures seem to question the adequacy of social, economic and political arrangements and institutions. Here one can argue that student activism is the result of social discontent in African societies.

In the four case studies, it is clear that, the most general hypothesis which has been repeatedly advanced to account for youth protest suggests that it is a result of a process set in motion by rapid rates of social change and the discrepancy between the formative experience of parental generations and those of a given generation of youth.

With the above views in mind, let us briefly examine the problems or issues that this project intended to address. The following sections on Zimbabwe, South Africa, Cameroon and Eritrea attempted to provide a general framework from which comparative research questions could be posed.

Higher Education and Student Politics in Zimbabwe

As in all other countries, students in Zimbabwe have been at the forefront of the democratization debate and process since colonial rule. Since the early 1990s, they have become more organized to respond to societal demands and to demand good governance by forging alliances with other civic groups. Changes in the political and economic environment played a significant role in shaping these attitudes. In the early 1980s, students rallied behind the government in the transformation phase after the long war of liberation and most of their energy was directed towards community service. In the late 1980s, prescriptions of the economic structural adjustment programme had begun to affect them and suspicions of government's intentions towards the student body began to arise. By 1989, the one-party state advocated by the government became the pivotal point of student activism. Students saw the government as reneging on hard-won democratic ideals, which was a clear betrayal of the liberation struggle. A major victory for the students was the crushing of the intended one party-state. This victory saw an increasing shift and emphasis on their part in questioning issues of national significance. Unfortunately, the postcolonial state turned into a 'cunning state' which sought persistently to constrain issues that deal with education. The current government hailed student activism during the struggle but it is seen to have systematically denied it space after independence. This marginalization has compelled students in higher learning institutions to organize and reclaim political space they had before. The study on Zimbabwe therefore critically analyses the nature and the role of student activism in Zimbabwe since 1980.

Throughout Zimbabwe's twenty-year democracy, students have functioned as an episodic opposition force, demonstrating against the government's policies which the public in general consider as a violation of their freedom and dignity at times in solidarity with whichever group has grievances against the government such as the workers or teachers but mostly for the improvement of their own conditions as students and their employment prospects. The various student movements or organisations at the tertiary institutions and the national students union have been avenues for political socialization since the mid-1980s. Many of the current political leaders were all active in the union and some students who aspire for political office still learn the tricks of the trade in the union. Of late, their slogan has become "change the world". That students are viewed as fighting for political space raises questions on whether the students' calls for change are merely instrumental.

In January 2002, the Students' Union General Council resolved to support the opposition party, the MDC, in its fight for democracy; not only because they desire freedom, but also because the president of the opposition had shown consistent support for the students since 1988 when he was a trade union leader. In 1989, he was arrested for issuing a public statement in support of student demonstrations. The pro-democracy role the students have played raises some questions which this project seeks to answer. To begin with, who are the students in these institutions and what are their aspirations both as individuals and in collectivity? How do students deal with tensions within the student body? How much space is there for female students to participate in student activities? How has the government responded to student activism over time and space? How does their activism compare with that of the students in the four countries? These are the questions the research attempts to address.

Transformation and Student Politics in South Africa

Higher education institutions provide youth with vital space in which to engage in transformative activism and to develop democratic citizenship. In South Africa's turbulent history, students, like in Zimbabwe, have played a critical role in social and political change – all too often attracting brutal and violent state repression. During the 1970s and 1980s, their sustained activism contributed significantly to turning the historical tide against apartheid. However, since the first democratic elections in 1994, which signalled the end of the political struggle against apartheid, conditions surrounding and within South Africa's higher education institutions have changed markedly. With this, the role and contribution of students in educational change have also changed. This study clearly documents these changes and identifies the constraints and opportunities surrounding student activism and citizenship in the current context of South African higher education.

As part of a comprehensive framework for transformation, the South African government's 1997 White Paper on Higher Education strongly promotes cooperative governance in higher education institutions. Against this backdrop, one of the key issues analysed in the South African case study concerns the effectiveness of student participation in the various governing structures at universities and technikons in South Africa.

One of the consequences of the 1997 White Paper, then, was the introduction of a form of representative democracy at higher education institutions. Accordingly, the research examines the two issues that emerged as centrally important in examining effective student participation: 1) Who represents students, that is, what is the profile of those students being elected as representatives, with regard to race, gender, age, undergraduate or postgraduate levels and fields of study? This is likely to have a bearing on the nature and efficacy of student participation. 2) What different patterns of formal representation and informal activities (such as lobbying, consultation and other practices) occurred within and around the various new governance structures at different institutions? How did students negotiate the constraints and opportunities within this to influence policy related processes? These patterns had a direct bearing on the effectiveness of student participation.

To examine these developments and their impact on student activism and democratic citizenship, the study attempted to describe and analyse key trends in student governance and SRC activities, since 1997, at three universities in the Western Cape region of South Africa.

These key trends include:

- patterns shaping student participation in structures of governance within universities and technikons,
- factors affecting the effectiveness of student participation in governance structures in universities and technikons, and
- the extent to which students influence decision-making processes in institutions.

Democratisation and Student Politics in Cameroon

Until 1993, higher education in Cameroon was principally restricted to Cameroon's single bilingual university – the University of Yaounde, albeit with university centres in Buea, Douala, Dschang and Ngaoundere. However, as a result of overcrowding and other factors, all the university centres were upgraded to full university status, and the University of Yaounde split into two separate institutions, thus bringing to six the number of state institutions of higher learning. As a result of the reform, the University of Buea became the only English-speaking university in the country where most of this study was conducted. The factors leading to this process are analysed in the case study of Cameroon.

The research in Cameroon focused on student politics or activism at the University of Buea. The objective, being to determine the character of student activism in this institution with a view to comparing it to student politics at the University of Yaounde just before the university reforms.

The research reveals that soon after the creation of the University of Buea, student politics galvanised around issues such as the university's demand for more financial commitment from students and the desire to run their affairs without interference from the university administration. In 1995, conflict between the student body and the university administration degenerated into violence on an unprecedented scale, leading to the burning of the registrar's car, the arbitrary and wanton arrests of students and the militarization of the campus for over a week. Student politics was also banned and the university became more or less, a replica of the one-party state, bereft of divergence, alternative or dissenting views. Since 1995, then, student politics at the University of Buea has been tailored to suit the whims and caprices of the administration that is largely state-appointed. What is similar or different about student activism in Buea when compared to cases in South Africa, Zimbabwe or Eritrea? Such are the issues that constitute a critical study of student activism at the University of Buea.

Post-war Instability and Student Politics in Eritrea

Higher education institutions provide youth with important space to make far-fetched claims on citizenship issues in the national political system. The state and society also place great expectations on students, especially higher education students, when it comes to nation-building and national transformation projects. Students have played a significant role in the history of national liberation in Eritrea. For example, student mobilization and demonstrations were instrumental in the 1960s in the revival of nationalist sentiments, and they have endowed the Eritrean people with the human resources for its political mobilization and the armed struggle. During this period, students of all social backgrounds voluntarily joined the struggle, contributing to the success of the struggle. After Eritrea gained independence in 1993, youths were at the centre of the nation's long-term projects. The Eritrean government felt the need to involve youths in nation-building and reconstruction projects. As part of such projects, the national service and summer work programmes for students were adopted and implemented in 1994. The national service was made compulsory for every Eritrean aged eighteen and above with 18 months earmarked for both military training and civic duty. The summer work programme for high school students was also launched. This annual programme targeted students involved in agricultural and educational development projects. Both were declared mandatory for all young citizens of Eritrea. Students have been and still are, actively involved in these national projects. Moreover, students rallied behind the government in the two-year border war with Ethiopia as far as going to the war fronts as soldiers. After the war had stopped in 2000 and peace agreements signed subsequently, the dynamics changed.

Students in Eritrea's only university, the university of Asmara, had gotten politically active in 2001. National programmes that had hitherto gone practically unchallenged in theory and practice came under criticism from the student body. However, in mid-June the student body openly objected to the usual summer work programme's mode of implementation and rationale. In so doing, they referred to international human rights conventions, citizenship rights and socio-economic problems. The university also served as a public platform for discussions on several issues. The issue was also discussed in the private newspapers that existed at the time. Concurrently, this period also witnessed a split in the government and the public media. Questions were raised and the stakes were high that there would be strong resistance among students following the government's imprisonment of the student president and forced movement of students into desert camps for the summer service. That decision was highly politicised and condemned as a blatant violation of human rights violations. No active students' movement existed thereafter. However, one significant effect of such activism was changing the nationalist pre-figurative political culture described by some people as a 'culture of silence'. A year after these incidents, we witnessed a silent political activism, not as a result of nationalist repertoires, but probably because of the repressive measures taken by the government to suppress student activism.

This case study, then, is a starting point for addressing the broad issues of citizenship, nationalism and life prospects and democratization among youth in higher education institutions. The short-lived student movement touched on such core issues as legitimacy, discourses and practices of citizenship and national identity in Eritrea. The study is a purposive sample survey conducted during the summer of 2003, two years after the collapse of the short-lived student movement of 2001. It investigates how student activism and perceptions of life prospects have responded to political processes between 1998 and 2003. The study explores student perceptions of their life plans, career choices and level activism. It unveils interesting patterns in students' perception that vary according to gender, generational and experiential differences of students. The study also looks into how students negotiate nationalist political repertoires in thinking about their current and future individual and social lives.

Research Objectives

The research project has the following specific objectives:
- To focus fieldwork on issues relating to higher education and student activism in selected universities in South Africa, Cameroon, Zimbabwe and Eritrea;
- To generate field data that can contribute and inform policy on higher education in Africa with regard to student activism;
- To compare the nature of student activism in various African countries and their significance in our understanding of higher education in Africa.

- To compare data on the social backgrounds and level of activism of students in selected countries, with a view to undertaking limited generalisation on the correlation between social backgrounds, university experiences and activism.

Research Questions

Some of the key questions that researchers were interested in are as follows:

- What precisely is student activism in the selected countries, in terms of mechanisms, strategies, etc.?
- Is student activism in Africa a passing phase, a permanent process or simply circumstantial?
- What patterns of political socialisation do student activists experience and how do these experiences shape or determine their levels of activism?
- How has student activism changed in relation to transformations within higher education structures or in relation to broader political changes (e.g. from one-party state to multiparty state, apartheid to democracy, liberal or social democracy to authoritarian rule, etc.)?
- What is specific or common to universities as spaces where students engage in political activism whose consequences extend beyond the university?

Relevance or Significance of the Study

Existing literature on higher education and student activism in Africa suffers from an acute shortage of comparatively informed approaches. As a result, this study reveals that research on student activism in Africa is grossly under-theorised and inadequate, hence the huge gap in the understanding of the processes, events, strategies, issues or debates that inform or characterise student activism across the continent. This study is, first and foremost, the modest contribution of some young scholars to the debate in a bid to understand student activism as a relevant component of higher education in Africa.

This volume will undoubtedly be of tremendous assistance to university. It is a rich collection of experiences which university administrators should consider in order to create a conducive learning environment on their various campuses. It may not be easy for universities, though, to meet the economic demands of their students. However, administration-students mutual understanding could be improved by genuine dialogue between the two pillars. As long as students are left out of the consultation process on some of the critical issues which affect the university, there will always be persistent tension on the campus. No amount of force will ever destroy this show of strength by students, since they feel they are part and parcel of a community which cherishes democratic values.

1. Cameroon

Student Activism, Violence and the Politics of Higher Education in Cameroon: A Case Study of the University of Buea (1993-2003)

Jude Fokwang

Introduction

In the morning of 3 February 2003, over 3000 students of the University of Buea (UB), Cameroon, took to the streets to express their discontent over rising insecurity in Molyko, the university residential area. This was the first major student protest since November 1995 (see below). The last student strike had resulted in the abolition of the students' union and a ban on student strike action. During the February 2003 protests, students expressed their outrage over recurrent armed robberies in their residential quarters. It had become public knowledge that a gang of armed bandits had repeatedly raided student quarters in Molyko, stealing cellphones, money, shoes and handbags. Some female students were also reported to have been raped. In the night of Monday 3 February, the alleged robbers descended once again on Molyko and broke into at least five student hostels. The news spread like wildfire and by 7 a.m., a considerable number of students had occupied and barricaded the main road to Buea town in protest. Life came to a standstill as traffic grounded to a halt, caused by the protesting students who blamed the civil authorities of Buea for failing to provide adequate security in the university neighbourhood. The students also blamed the police for failing to intervene whenever major robberies were reported. They maintained that they had had enough of the the police's excuses.

Exasperated by the most recent robbery and police ineptitude, the students resolved to march to the Governor's Office to plead their case. The governor, alerted of the unrest, decided to pacify the protesting students. On his way, he met the riotous students, who requested that he accompanied them on foot to the site of the recent burglary. His refusal further enraged the students. Some of them started throwing stones at the governor's car, thus provoking the police to use tear gas in order to disperse the huge crowd. The students remained defiant and only returned to campus at midday, threatening to take the law into their own hands.[1] A few weeks later, one of the presumed bandits was identified and a mob of students fell on him and 'necklaced' him at the popular university junction. As he painfully burnt to death, the crowd stood by and watched, delighted to have exercised popular justice.

The strike yielded some dividends. A police post was created in the Molyko neighbourhood and a 9 p.m.–to–6 a.m. curfew was imposed.[2] The curfew infuriated the students who alleged that the police were using the restriction as an excuse to intimidate students returning from night classes or study periods. It was also reported that the governor was relieved of his post shortly after the strike. Although he may have been dismissed for 'political' reasons, students insisted that the main reason was his inability to address security problems in the student quarters.

The above account provides a rough idea of the nature of student activism in contemporary Cameroon. In this specific case, we encounter a group of nameless and faceless students occupying a particular constituency in society – as university students who, by means of a violent strike action, assert and claim their rights to state protection as young citizens. Youths' appropriation of violence as a means of collective action has contributed to a kind of moral panic. Indeed, they are sometimes described as 'terrors of the present' (Comaroff and Comaroff 2001:33) on account of their propensity for violent action. But who precisely are these students? What are their various claims both as individuals and as groups? What is their relationship to university authorities, the civil administration and the state? What are the implications of their activism? In the light of the above questions, I examine student activism at the University of Buea by locating its 'politics' within a broader analytic framework which incorporates the struggle for the democratisation of the state and institutions of higher learning in Cameroon. The key issue explored is student activism's responses to transformations within higher education structures and broader political processes between 1990 and 2003. Furthermore, I explore the 'university' as a setting for various kinds of student activism whose consequences reach beyond the university. I argue that student activism cannot be depoliticised because it is, by its very nature, political. I make a distinction between student activism in the early and mid-1990s and the situation in 2003 when the fieldwork for this chapter was conducted. The divergence is explained by a range of factors such as generational and experiential differences, as well as transformations in the political economy of Cameroon.

Through this analysis, I hope to make a contribution to on-going efforts by scholars and policy-makers towards understanding the socio-political status of higher education in Africa and student participation in the management of these institutions. This analysis also has implications for appreciating the dynamics of democratic processes and political culture in postcolonial Cameroon.

A Brief History of the University of Buea

The University of Buea (UB), located in the South West Province, is a leading state-sponsored university in Cameroon. It has reported the highest success rates among its student population, compared to other state universities in the country. While a number of private universities have cropped up in the English-speaking Cameroonian provinces, especially in the North West Province, UB remains the only official anglophone state university. The other five state universities are, in the main, francophone, although the University of Yaounde 1 is nominally bilingual. UB's student population as of 2003 was about 7,000 and it continues to attract students from the two anglophone provinces and more recently, from the francophone Cameroonian provinces.

Higher education started in Cameroon in 1961, following the establishment of the National Institute for University Studies in Yaounde. In 1962, the Institute was renamed the Federal University of Cameroon (Njeuma et al 1999:2), a shift intended to reflect the political climate of that era. The English colony of Southern Cameroons had gained its independence in October 1961 by joining the already independent Republic of Cameroon to form a federation. In 1967, the Federal University of Cameroon became the University of Yaounde and enjoyed a monopoly until 1993. Between 1967 and 1993, the university had outgrown its capacity, owing to overpopulation on a campus that was originally designed for 5,000 students. In 1993, for instance, the student population of the University of Yaounde was over 40,000 (Njeuma et al 1999:1) with extremely limited resources to cater for the growing number of students. The establishment of four university centres in 1977[3] alleviated the deplorable situation only for a short period. One of the main problems of the University of Yaounde was that its programmes replicated in structure and content those of the French university system, thus limiting access to anglophone students (cf. Njeuma et al 1999:10; also see Konings 2002). It was against this background that anglophone Cameroonians repeatedly demanded the establishment of an English-oriented university for the anglophone population, as most anglophones had to go to neighbouring Nigeria for university studies (cf. Nyamnjoh 1996).

Eventually, Decree No. 92/074 of 13 April 1992 formally elevated all the university centres to full-fledged universities. Hence, the Buea University Centre became the University of Buea 'conceived in the Anglo-Saxon tradition [...] consistent with the education system prevailing in Anglophone primary and secondary schools' (Njeuma et al. 1999:10). Dr Dorothy Njeuma, a renowned administrator and prominent member of the ruling party was appointed vice-chancellor by another presidential decree. She held the position until September 2005 when she was transferred to the University of Yaounde I. One of the positive consequences of the university reforms of 1993 was that the creation of more state universities increased access by female students. For instance, by 1999, 47 per cent of students at UB were female and some informants estimated that this might have increased to about fifty-one per cent.

Lectures officially started at the University of Buea on 10 May 1993 with an enrolment of 786 students.[4] Most of them were anglophone students who had been transferred from the University of Yaounde. The number rose to over 4,000 by 1995 and has steadily increased since then. Students were expected to pay a registration fee of 50,000 CFA (then about US$200 but currently about US$85 owing to the devaluation of the local currency in January 1994). Since 1993, the University of Buea has provided exemplary training to its students, compared to the other state universities, despite a series of turbulent student protests against university authorities, the first of which started just three months after the commencement of official lectures.

Student Activism at the University of Buea from 1993 to 1995

UB was established at the peak of the economic crisis in Cameroon. In 1993, civil servants' salaries were slashed by sixty per cent followed by a fifty per cent devaluation of the currency in January 1994.[5] Many government employees went without salaries for over three months. The socio-political landscape was characterised by periodic moments of civil disobedience. The economy was yet to recover from the ghost town operations[6] that took place between 1991 and 1992, during which economic activities almost came to a halt especially in Cameroon's economic capital, Douala. In fact, the establishment of more state universities in a context of acute economic crisis was criticised by the Bretton Woods institutions as counter-productive (Njeuma *et al* 1999). It was during this economic turmoil that UB was born. According to then Vice-chancellor, Dorothy Njeuma, at its inception in 1993, the university received no financial support from the government. Even before the higher education reforms were implemented, she argues, the institution had not received the government grant allocated to university centres for the 1992/93 fiscal year.[7]

It was precisely this desperate economic situation that prompted the government to introduce registration fees in 1993. Prior to this, students at the University of Yaounde received regular scholarships from the state, and did not have to pay tuition fees, except a registration fee of 3,500 CFA. The higher education reforms eventually ushered in more state universities and the payment of a higher registration fee by students, which has been maintained at 50,000 CFA per annum. Although students at the University of Yaounde protested against this new decision, clashing with university authorities and the government (cf. Konings 2003), there is general consensus that the newly transferred students at UB were quite willing to pay the required fees. Most anglophones interpreted this as their direct support for the newly established 'Anglo-Saxon' institution.

Three months after UB became a full-fledged university, it experienced its first student strike. At issue was an alleged increase in student registration fees. News had circulated around campus that during the next academic year, students in the Faculties of Arts and Social Sciences would pay 150,000 CFA while their counterparts in the Faculty of Science would pay 200,000 CFA (then about US$600 and US$800 respectively). On 20 August 1993, the students went on strike to express their discontent over the alleged decision. The protests led to the disruption of the semester exams that had been scheduled for late August. Although the strike was non-violent, soldiers and policemen were unexpectedly deployed on campus to keep an eye on students.[8] Students refused to write their exams unless the university administration rescinded its threat to increase fees. They also used this opportunity to voice their dissatisfaction over other issues such as the high cost of living in student quarters. In particular, they complained of the high rents imposed on them by landlords eager to make quick profits from the growing student population. While the university authorities and the student leaders remained at loggerheads over the strike, the Minister of Higher Education intervened and denied that the government had any plans to introduce tuition fees at UB. Eventually the students called off the strike and wrote their exams.

This incident provoked intense discussions among ordinary citizens and students. Some observers were of the opinion that the student protest could have been averted if the university authorities had dialogued constructively with student leaders. Instead, each side had accused the other of bad faith, thus leaving little or no room for constructive dialogue. It should be pointed out that at its inception, UB encouraged the formation of a democratically elected students' union to represent the concerns of the student body. Authorities also insinuated that UB was the first state university in Cameroon to provide the students' union with a seat on the University Council.[9] It was during one of such council meetings that the students' union president, Ebenezar Akwanga, was alleged to have rejected the idea of increasing student registration fees. During the strike, the registrar of UB purportedly asked the students' union president to set up a delegation to present their grievances to the vice-chancellor, but the student leader rejected the request. In an interview with *The Herald*, he gave the following explanation for refusing to meet the vice-chancellor:

"What she failed to realise was that she was appointed and I was elected. I am representing my constituency – the student body. Since the students don't want me to have any dialogue with her at this moment until she carries out their demand, I was not supposed to constitute a delegation to meet her. It is just like parliamentarians; you cannot act without the approval of your constituency".[10]

Not everybody agreed with the student leader. Some students reportedly accused Mr Akwanga of being arrogant and having refused to make use of the opportunity to plead the case of the student community. Others accused him of writing a rude letter to the vice-chancellor, thus misconstruing his lack of diplomatic skills for heroism. Ngwesse Nkwelle, a reporter for *The Herald* described the students as 'too young to have known anything else, especially about how to channel discontent'. This view notwithstanding, it was apparent that students were a force to reckon with and that there was need for more democratic leeway for dialogue between activists and the authorities.

Unfortunately, this was not the case as the vice-chancellor in a show of autocratic power, resolved to ban further strikes by students and compelled them to sign an undertaking never to strike against university authorities. This requirement was fixed as a condition for registration by returning students. Among other stipulations, Article 2 of the document published on 7 September 1993 stipulated that the undersigned student would 'abstain from any form of strike action whatsoever and from any activity likely to jeopardize the smooth functioning of any of the establishments of the university'.[11]

Many students reacted angrily to this injunction although they eventually signed the document. In fact, students were expected to sign the undertaking together with their parents or guardians prior to completing registration formalities. Some students were of the opinion that the vice-chancellor had banned further strikes in order to pre-empt student outrage if tuition fees were increased during the next academic year scheduled to commence in November 1993.

Upon returning to UB for the 1993/1994 academic year, students also learnt of the shocking decision by the vice-chancellor to dissolve the students' union executive headed by Mr Akwanga. The latter and his colleagues were accused by the administration of the following:

- misleading the student body to commit serious acts of indiscipline, including the boycott of examinations from August 23 to 25 1993, barricading the gates and access roads to the university thereby disrupting activities, threatening students and staff, and insulting staff;
- refusal to meet the authorities despite repeated invitations to do so;
- rude and insulting attitude of the president and other members of the executive towards the administration;
- participation in activities likely to jeopardize the smooth functioning of the university.[12]

They were also banned from running in future elections or holding any office on campus for one year. Although this decision did not trigger off a new strike, many students condemned the vice-chancellor's decision as undemocratic and ruthless. They also threatened not to elect a new students' union government.

Although the student leaders were divested of *de jure* authority, they apparently continued to enjoy some legitimacy and still influenced student activities informally. For instance, students threatened to strike again during the registration period in early November 1993. According to a student circular, a peaceful demonstration was scheduled to hold on campus on 4 November 1993 following the administration's request that students should pay 2,000 CFA for students' union fees. Students argued that they had paid 2,000 CFA during the previous academic year and the funds had not been used. They interpreted the request to pay another students' union fee as dubious and exploitative. Furthermore, many argued that without a students' union government, they could consider the union dead. The timely intervention of the registrar pre-empted the strike, owing to an official decision from his office annulling the dues.[13]

During the 1994/1995 academic year, the university administration, in a bid to stave off its financial crisis, conceived the idea of a Parent Faculty Association (PFA) modeled on the Parent Teacher Associations (PTA) that are part and parcel of primary and secondary school management in anglophone Cameroon. The PFA was designed to co-opt parents into the management of the university and to create awareness of the need to diversify the university's sources of income instead of depending exclusively on the government. To this end, each student was required to pay a PFA fee of 20,000 CFA per academic year. News about the plan to introduce the PFA fee spread quite rapidly as students were about to conclude their semester exams in June 1995. A newly elected students' union (see below) interpreted this as the administration's strategy to increase fees. The union leaders proceeded to mobilise the student population against the idea, again pitting students against the administration in defiance of the ban on student strikes. During the protest, the students confronted the newly elected president of the PFA, Mr Fossung and Dr Biaka, the secretary general, forcing them to resign. Shortly after this incident, the PFA was dissolved by an order of the Minister of Higher Education.

While the student protest succeeded in its objective, it led to unexpected consequences for several students. Five students, three of them from the Department of Journalism and Mass Communication, were suspended indefinitely for inciting students to strike. Some of the students had written articles critical of the administration in the student newspaper, *The Chariot*. The paper was suspended after the strike. When it was permitted to resume two years later, a new editor was appointed and the Journalism department was requested to redefine the objectives of the paper.

Sometime around June 1995, a student memo posted on bill boards on and off campus and signed by one of the suspended students, Cho Lucas Ayaba, accused the administration of being anti-Anglo-Saxon in its handling of student crises. The memo cited, among other things, the administration's arbitrary suspension of students for peaceful demonstration, the undemocratic dissolution of the first students' union executive and the unilateral decision to charge an additional 20,000 CFA as PFA dues.[14] The suspended students called on their colleagues not to pay the alleged PFA fees and to continue to fight for a democratic university administration.

At the end of the 1994/1995 academic year, a new students' union executive was elected into office, thus reviving the union that had been suspended during the previous year. Students were excited about the revived union and anticipated that the union leaders would effectively articulate their problems. However, it appeared that the administration was already biased against the new leaders in view of the role they had played in the protest against the PFA.

The revived students' union known as the University of Buea Students Union (UBSU) went into effect in September 1995, at the beginning of the 1995/96 academic year. One of its first achievements was to open and run a student canteen which provided photocopy services at reduced rates compared to other private agents on campus. The new leaders appeared to be quite dynamic and popular among students. But they soon got into trouble with the authorities over a range of issues, the most critical being the administration's reluctance to give them access to student funds. The union leaders claimed that although they had met the budgetary and constitutional requirements for such access, the UB authorities had no plans to collaborate with them. They threatened to call a general student strike on Monday, 27 November 1995.

On 24 November 1995, UBSU submitted a memorandum to the vice-chancellor and the registrar, enumerating student grievances, namely: the administration's reluctance to give union leaders access to the students' union account; the urgent need of funds to run the student canteen for the welfare of the students; the university's refusal to grant permission to UBSU to publish its newsletter, *UBSU Time* and the exclusion of union leaders from the decision-making process in matters affecting students.[15] This memorandum led to a deterioration in the already hostile relations between UB authorities and the new union leaders.

After receiving the memorandum, the registrar immediately sealed off the student canteen and asked the union leaders to vacate their offices without further delay. Shortly thereafter, the president and secretary-general of UBSU were served with a letter from the vice-chancellor suspending them indefinitely. According to Dr Dorothy Njeuma, the student leaders were suspended for 'gross indiscipline, disrespect for authorities and incitement of students to revolt... [and consequently were] barred from entering the campus of the University of Buea and from any services offered by the institution until further notice.[16] Later that afternoon, the university was in a state of turmoil as students came out to protest against what they interpreted as the dismissal of their student leaders. Their main objective was the immediate reversal of the vice-chancellor's decision, failing which they would continue to boycott classes until their demands were met. The entrance to the university was barricaded and students marched back and forth chanting freedom songs. Thus, a strike that had been planned for 27 November, unexpectedly began earlier and took a new and violent turn. As more and more students joined their protesting colleagues, the protests moved from campus to the main streets in Buea, thus disrupting traffic and normal business.

The demonstrations turned violent when the students set the registrar's car on fire. According to eyewitnesses, the registrar had tried to force his way into the university campus in defiance of the barricades erected by students. Unable to drive through the huge rocks that had been rolled into the street, the registrar came out of his car to confront the students. But he was chased away and his car set to flames. Other acts of violence were also reported such as the burning of the UBSU vice-president's apartment allegedly in retaliation for his pro-administration stance.[17]

News of the burning of the registrar's car spread throughout the town. A crisis that had started as a standoff between students and the university administration soon degenerated into an ethnic conflict. Members of the Bakweri ethnic group, who are autochthonous to Buea, soon began to attack 'strangers'. Although no casualties were reported, students were appalled to learn that their strike against the university authorities had been appropriated by indigenous ethnic groups to suit their own purposes. Apparently, the union president, Mr Valentine Nti, was a member of an ethnic group in the North West Province while the vice-president and secretary-general were from the South West Province. The strike was therefore interpreted as a rebellion of North West students against the Bakweri-dominated authorities of the university.

As the strike gathered momentum, soldiers were called into the campus and student quarters in Molyko. This provoked even more violence as students resorted to throwing stones at the gendarmes and soldiers – *intifada* style. Students also burnt tyres on the streets and pulled more rocks to block the main streets. Inflamed by this open show of confrontation, the military became even more brutal. They broke into apartments and arrested students. Many were savagely beaten and hundreds more were taken to police cells. The military crackdown on the protests forced the students to retreat. After four days of demonstrations and fierce confrontation with the 'forces of state violence', many students began to desert their quarters for neighbouring towns. It was only after a week that uneasy peace was restored.

A major consequence of the strike was the reinstatement of the ban on student politics at UB, which created an even wider rift between the administration and the student body. More students were reported to have been dismissed, particularly from the Department of Journalism, on the grounds that they had published articles in private newspapers considered injurious to the reputation of the university. Intimidation and various forms of administrative harassment were employed by the authorities to rein in students. Eventually, the authorities resolved to reinstate the the secretary-general of the defunct students' union in his post, but the union president's suspension was maintained and he was prevented from enrolling in any state university in Cameroon, thus compelling him to seek alternative opportunities in exile. In the aftermath of the strike, the university community was subjected to police-style discipline. Even lecturers who spoke against the authorities were labelled as subversive and targeted for arbitrary punitive sanctions. Four years later, in 1999, students were allowed once again to organise themselves into a student government. This time, the administration had finally devised a blueprint to keep students permanently divided and, therefore, subject to further control and disciplinary power.

Students' Union Politics since 1999

In this section, I examine the form and content of student politics since its reintroduction in 1999. I argue that the employment of divide-and-rule tactics by the university authorities to make students toe the line is largely inspired by existing methods designed and refined by the Biya regime.[18] Thus, mimicry of the post-colony in farcical proportions is reproduced at the micro-level of the university leading to continuous erosion of the limited democratic space that had been gained at the inception of the university.

After the ruthless abolition of the students' union in 1995 and the arbitrary dismissal of the students' union president, students had no form of collective or central representation through which they could channel their concerns. Although each class had its elected delegates (known as class delegates), their legitimacy was limited to their specific departments and more particularly to their class. While a central students' union was visibly absent, many student associations continued to thrive and tended to organise their activities along academic and socio-cultural lines. Between 1995 and 1999, there was no organised demand for a revival of a common students' union most probably for fear of administrative reprisals. Another reason was the generational and experiential gap between students who enrolled in 1993 and those who came much later at the turn of the decade. The pioneer students were already acquainted with political activism on account of their experiences at the University of Yaounde prior to their transfer to Buea. Students who enrolled later knew little about students' union activism except for the legendary accounts of union leaders who had been dismissed or suspended by authorities for daring to think differently. The re-introduction of student government four years after its suspension could also be an indication of careful timing by the authorities – on the assumption that most of the students who were part of the student riots between 1993 and 1995 would have graduated.

It is against this backdrop that one can understand the nature of student activism after 1995. In typical patrimonial style, the re-introduction of student government was interpreted in many circles as an expression of the largesse and goodwill of the vice-chancellor towards the students. But the structure of its organisation was completely bereft of student input. Rather, it was unilaterally imposed on them and all they had to do was to comply with the dictates of the university administration. Instead of a common students' union as seen in most universities the world over, the university authorities devised a new system of student representative government whose power and functions were restricted to individual faculties.

According to the genius of the authorities, each of the five faculties constituted a separate and distinct constituency. Each of the faculties elected its own executive whose jurisdiction was limited to the faculty and, as such, was unable to speak on behalf of the entire student body. The five faculty presidents made up what was popularly termed the 'college of presidents' and when this study was conducted in 2003, the president of the Faculty of Social and Management Sciences had been elected as spokesperson of the College of Presidents. As leader of the college of presidents, he claimed the right to speak on behalf of the entire student population, but in reality, his legitimacy did not extend beyond his faculty. While this structure conveyed the idea of the existence of a decentralised student government, many students felt that the numerous faculty student governments were toothless bulldogs since their powers were extremely limited. Some students perceived the presidents and other office-holders as mere stooges of the authorities, partly because they were inefficient in their respective domains and, as a 'college of presidents', unable to forge a common agenda representative of the plight of the wider student community.

Each Faculty Association (FA) had a 12-member executive. All the associations were subject to a common constitution (drawn up by the authorities) outlining the pattern and functions of the student governments. Their funds were collectively controlled by the university administration and each executive was accountable directly to the dean of its faculty and ultimately to the vice-chancellor. Membership was open to all full-time registered students upon payment of their students' union fee, which had to be paid in full prior to registration.

The faculty associations operated under the ideology of peaceful co-existence with the university authorities. In this regard, dialogue was the one and only acceptable maxim, reiterated to me time and again by the student leaders. In fact, it was mandatory for students to sign an undertaking not to strike or protest against the administration as already highlighted. While dialogue was often cited as the paramount ideology, the reality was that student representatives were often treated as extensions of the administrative machinery rather than as partners representing a different constituency perhaps with different interests.

Legitimacy of New Student Leaders

Since the introduction of the new system of student government, the leaders have enjoyed relatively little or no legitimacy. All the FA presidents were males and most of them claimed to have held positions of leadership in high school. Some of them were also office-holders in other youth associations such as alumni or cultural organisations. While most of them expressed interest in national politics, none of them were members of any political party.

The student leaders were generally eclipsed by the leaders and activities of other student associations, particularly famous alumni organisations of prestigious high schools such as St. Joseph's College, Sacred Heart College, Presbyterian Secondary School Mankon and Saker Baptist College. Alumni associations which were independent groups had no relationship with the administration and were perceived by students as playing a more dominant role in student life than in FAs.

Corruption among faculty presidents was also widespread. Although none of the leaders I met in 2003 were accused of corrupt practices, it was an open secret that most of the leaders who came to power in 1999 and 2000 were responsible for the mismanagement of student funds. In October 2001, for instance, UB authorities were shocked to learn of the alleged malpractices of the student leader of the Faculty of Social and Management Sciences. The leader claimed to have donated a substantial amount of money to *The Chariot* as support from his executive, but *The Chariot* denied receiving any funds from the infamous president. His degree was withheld by the university because he could not account for the funds. The authorities appear to have withheld the degrees of several student leaders accused of mismanaging student funds. However, the authorities have failed to bring charges against the student embezzlers and many students are sceptical of and indifferent to the issue of corruption among student leaders.

Many interviewees felt that their colleagues competed for the office of president in FAs purely for financial gain. Others charged that they were concerned about the criteria used in selecting candidates, since this was controlled by the administration. According to many participants, the university authorities ought not to participate in the selection of candidates and the conduct of FA elections. This claim emerged on account of the suspicion that the authorities selected students who were perceived to be pliant. On the other hand, the authorities maintained that candidates were selected on academic merit. In response, students asserted that smarter students did not necessarily make better leaders and that every student ought to be given a chance.

This assertion went hand-in-hand with the claim that most student leaders were in league with the administration and lacked the capacity to defend the interests of the student community. For instance, the university has a contrived, perhaps mimicked, tradition of presenting New Year wishes to the vice-chancellor. During one of these banal exercises, a student leader was chosen by the administration to present a speech on behalf of his colleagues. He applied himself to the task and prepared a fine speech for the occasion. But a few minutes before he delivered the speech, he was presented with an alternative 'official speech' by the Director of Student Affairs which he read to the vice-chancellor and her collaborators with a feigned gusto.

It also emerged from my interviews that none of the student leaders represented the student community at senate meetings, despite official provision for a student seat. No wonder, over sixty per cent of students surveyed said they were not satisfied with the performance of their student leaders. Most respondents claimed they did not know the specific functions of the faculty presidents other than the fact that they enjoyed the prestige of being called 'president' by ordinary students.

Student participation in various FAs was terribly low. Although there are competing theories for the discouraging level of participation, most students pointed out that it was a waste of time to attend FA meetings because nothing good came out of them. All the incumbent faculty presidents whom I interviewed conceded that student participation was very low. In the Faculty of Social and Management Sciences with a student population of over 4,000 the average attendance at FA meetings was 25. The same situation was true of the Faculty of Science with over 2,000 students. Females were least interested in FA politics. Many of them perceived it as a male domain and felt that they stood to gain nothing by devoting their time to FA affairs. During the last student elections, a female candidate in the Faculty of Social and Management Sciences dropped out of the race just before the commencement of the elections on the grounds that she felt intimidated. Since FAs were introduced, only the Faculty of Arts has had a female president. Although she completed her degree in the summer of 2002 and continued to live in the Molyko neighbourhood, she was still actively involved in the FA affairs of the Faculty of Arts owing to the absence of an elected executive for the 2002-2003 academic year.

Relationship Between Students and the Administration

There was a broad consensus among research participants that the relationship between the administration and the student community was not cordial. Students insisted that the administration's attitude was characterised by benign neglect and, sometimes, outright hostility. They also complained about a range of issues that had been continuously raised with the authorities for a couple of years, but which had not been addressed, despite promises to address them.

Many students were outraged by the lack of schedules for make-up examinations during the summer vacation. At issue was the fact that a large proportion of final year students had to spend an entire year repeating a course that could have been validated if resits were scheduled during the long holidays. Students complained that the other state universities in the country organized resits for all courses except the University of Buea. Students felt they needed an explanation from the authorities as to why most courses were not offered during summer make-up exam sessions.

Another key concern which students claimed the university authorities had failed to address was the problem of housing and insecurity in the student quarters. As highlighted earlier, the university provides accommodation to only about a hundred and twenty students on campus. Thus, about 7,000 students lived off-campus in private rooms whose rents are negotiated with landlords. There are no laws to protect tenants and this leads to arbitrary increases in rents by landlords desperate for quick profit. Most students felt the university authorities had the powers to reach an understanding with landlords granting that precedents had been established at the University of Ngaoundere in the Adamawa Province of Cameroon.

Students also complained of insecurity in their neighbourhood. Neither the university nor civil authorities in Buea had taken their complaints seriously. It was only after repeated armed robberies and a student protest that civil administrators decided to intervene to try and resolve the crisis. The creation of a police post in the student neighbourhood of Molyko was perceived to be largely ineffective by most students for a number of reasons. The police post was understaffed, and instead of keeping the peace, the police were allegedly more interested in stopping taxi drivers to extort bribes from them. There were reports of armed robberies during the period of my research and students expressed disappointment that no arrests had been made. The police, students affirmed, usually showed up only after the bandits had left the scene of the crime. An alternative solution, some students proposed, was for landlords to hire private security agents to patrol student residences, but this of course comes with a price tag. And it was apparent that students could not afford additional costs, which simply compounded their disillusionment with government authorities.

Another grievance expressed by many students was the university authorities' perceived lack of commitment to expand infrastructure., They complained in particular of overcrowding in lecture halls, limited access to potable water on campus (water was available in the university restaurant only) and defective toilet facilities. Some of the student leaders contended that they had approached the authorities with a student-sponsored proposal to install taps in selected parts of the campus but this proposal had been rejected. Despite these problems, the university built a new lecture hall in 2002 and gradually increased its library and staff infrastructure. In addition, a new building was constructed to house the Faculty of Social and Management Sciences. However, it should also be underscored that despite favourable attempts to expand infrastructure, the university's student-intake rate far outweighs the limited facilities. A campus that was built to accommodate just over 2,000 students currently has over 7,000 students and this number continues to increase every year. Students felt that the university had the resources but had allocated them to projects that were not perceived to benefit the student population. The construction of a fence round the university in 1999 was a case in point.

The university's decision to construct a fence touched off an unprecedented controversy among students, lecturers and even ordinary citizens. The project cost tens of millions of CFA. According to university officials, the fence was a top priority owing to the gradual encroachment on their land by private landlords. Many students were of the opinion that more lecture theatres and laboratories ought to be constructed instead of a fence. There was no open student protest against this project but an expatriate volunteer lecturer of sociology in the Faculty of Social and Management Sciences criticised the idea. Dr Kai Schmidt-Soltau, the said sociologist, spoke overtly against the project and labelled the fence a 'Cage of Fools' in one of his columns in a popular newspaper, *The Post*.

Dr Schmidt-Soltau eventually had an opportunity to raise his criticism in an academic audience during an august event on campus organised by a vibrant and popular student association known as the Organisation of African Unity (OAU) Club. The club was chaired by a final-year sociology major, whose pan-Africanist ideas had attracted much attention among students and faculty. During celebrations commemorating the African Union day, the OAU Club invited various personalities including the vice-chancellor, the Governor of the South West Province, human rights activists and several scholars at the university. Dr Schmidt-Soltau was also invited to present a talk to the club members and unknowingly to its organisers, he chose to speak on the topic of conflict resolution in Africa, with specific reference to the most contentious issue of the day – the construction of the fence. Alarmed by the sociologist's no-nonsense approach, the vice-chancellor accompanied by the governor stormed out of the hall during the lecture. A few days later, Dr Schmidt-Soltau was served with a letter terminating his voluntary services at the University of Buea. He was further forbidden to come within 500 metres of the university premises (cf. Schmidt-Soltau 1999). The authorities also intimidated the leaders of the OAU Club and threatened to dismiss its president for allowing their association to be used by 'subversive' individuals for private ends. A rival club was eventually formed under the auspices of the administration and this led to the collapse of the original OAU Club.

Students lamented the repressive disposition of the university administration, particularly the vice-chancellor. Such repression targeted not only students perceived as being 'subversive' but also lecturers who dared to criticise the administration or its stooges. For instance, university lecturers who openly called for better working conditions at the university were targeted for punitive sanctions (cf. Nyamnjoh and Jua 2002).

Censorship was also rife in the lone student newspaper, *The Chariot*. University lecturers who were back-stage members of the editorial board tended to censor news stories that were critical of university authorities. It should also be noted that *The Chariot* had been suspended for about two years following the student strike of June 1994. Hence the presence of lecturers on the editorial board tended to discourage students from publishing the kinds of stories they felt would be of interest to the student community. For example, *The Chariot* could not publish a news story about a university administrator who was accused of having swindled funds intended for a specific student activity because the censors perceived such news stories as provocative.

Research participants talked about the presence of spies. Many students alleged that the university authorities sponsored students as spies to monitor the activities of other students. Certain lecturers had also been co-opted as spies to monitor both students and their colleagues for subversive activities. Many interviewees expressed their outrage about the university's ban on students' right to strike or organise protests against the administration. This was interpreted as outright repression and the university authorities were challenged to vindicate their purported espousal of democratic culture by repealing the legislation which required students to sign a legal undertaking not to organise strikes or protest marches. In the next section, I make use of these findings to address a range of issues concerning violence, student politics and its relationship to broader political issues.

Violent Protests and the Contours of Repression

In the above paragraphs, I have provided a detailed account of student activism at the University of Buea since its inception in 1993. I have shown that student protests tended to be violent, an aspect which if considered more broadly, is not unique to students. Many scholars writing about student activism have recorded the crisis of violence that often accompanies most protests (see for example, Naidoo 1991; Wise 1998; Konings 2002; Mashayekhi 2001; Klopp & Orina 2002). Because many youth and student protests have often culminated in violence, 'young people are now seen and constructed as a menace' (Diouf 2003:9). Little effort is made to put acts of violence into perspective granting that student protesters are already categorised as 'les enfants terribles'. It is against this background that I wish to examine students' violent protests from a sociological perspective.

More often than not, most government officials perceive 'street protest as a form of deviant behaviour' (Aelst and Walgrave 2001:461). However, while some forms of protest have become normalised, others (such as violent protests) are subject to renewed stigmatisation. That notwithstanding, Apter (1997) asserts that 'people do not commit political violence without discourse' and such discursive constructions should be privileged in the analysis of violent protests. For instance, in the case of student protests at UB, one observes that actors were concerned with issues that went beyond often-repeated struggles for bread and butter. Student leaders tended to construct discourses around issues regarding their exclusion from decision-making processes and the administration's plans to exploit the student population. While these discourses did not espouse violence as a 'reordering' mechanism (cf. Apter 1997:5), students often resorted to violent protests as a means outside the rules of the game, and because of their efficacy in particular instances, they were legitimised and normalised among student activists. Hence violent protests could be viewed not only as a therapy by striking students but also as 'testimonials to moral claims – claims to a higher legitimacy, rectifying, that is, the righting of perceived injustices...' (Apter 1997:18). A case in point was the capture and ruthless necklacing of one of the alleged bandits in February 2003 at the Buea University junction. The government's silence over the issue could also be interpreted as an implicit acknowledgement of certain extra-institutional protests or forms of justice.[19]

Violent protests at UB could also be located within the realm of 'low politics' following Bayart's classic distinction between high and low politics. According to him, the sphere of low politics is occupied by marginalized groups such as women, children and the youth. To study low politics is to study the 'politics of the powerless' (cf. Cruise O'Brien 1996). But powerlessness does not entail the absence of agency granting that youth participation in the public sphere is contingent on different kinds of agency (cf. Durham 2000). Resort to violent protests by student activists has been interpreted as a form of deconstructing the state (Cruise O'Brien 1996) and perhaps as a way of 'uprooting' postcolonial legitimacies (Diouf 2003:7). This understanding could be extended to many African universities whose leadership in some cases represent the entrenched patrimonial state structures (see Klopp & Orina 2002 for similarities in Kenya). Thus, even in their perceived powerlessness, student protests at UB could be understood not only as addressing concerns relevant to their immediate circumstances, but also as confronting broader issues endemic to the body politic of the post-colony. The burning down of the registrar's car during the strike of November 1995 or the students' insistence that the governor of the South West Province should accompany them 'on foot' to the raided student hostels are statements of deconstruction. The semiotic contrast between the burnt 'car' and the everyday challenge of being a pedestrian is eloquent. By urging the governor to accompany the young citizens on foot, the students were actively uprooting or demystifying the fetishism which power has come to represent to many postcolonial government auxiliaries.

In a discussion of violence in the post-colony, one cannot afford to ignore the various forms of violence exercised by the postcolonial state against its citizens and in this case, the students at the University of Buea. According to Nyamnjoh and Jua (2002) 'education in Africa, from colonial times to the postcolony, has been the victim of various forms of violence, the most devastating of which is the violence of cultural and political conversion....' The African university has become a site of both academic and political repression whereby academics in league with the patrimonial state enjoy the 'license to use and abuse students' without remorse (Nyamnjoh and Jua 2002:5; also see Mbembe 1992, 2001, on the predicament of female students in male-dominated institutions of higher learning). The dynamics of the above claims could be examined more critically at the University of Buea where extreme and often arbitrary forms of violence have been employed by both the state and university authorities over students. In this connection, Foucault's concept of disciplinary power is useful as a model for understanding symbolic violence at UB. Disciplinary power is a form of surveillance internalised by people who represent the targets of power. The basic goal of disciplinary power is to produce a person who is docile and complacent with the system (Dreyfus and Rabinow 1985:134-135). To this end, 'disciplinary technologies' are employed to police and produce docile bodies. Writing about youth politics in postcolonial Africa, Mbembe (1985) noted some of the techniques of discipline utilized by postcolonial governments to police university students and the youth in general. He asserted that the techniques included among other things, the dissolution of student organisations and arrest of student leaders, forced labour for purposes of re-education, and the creation of rival student associations (Mbembe 1985:109-10). At the University of Buea, a range of these techniques have been used time after time and by every indication, the tempo of student politics at UB seems to have succumbed to a level of docility expected by the authorities. New students and perceived subversive activists are harassed and reminded of the fate of pioneer students who ended up in suspension lists because they dared to stand up to the authorities. The deployment of spies among both students and lecturers evokes the presence of a 'panopticon' or in popular parlance, the spectre of 'big brother'.

A familiar discourse often invoked by authorities to dismiss student claims is that the latter have been 'misled' or manipulated by agents who intend to destabilise the state (Mbembe 1985:110). It is quite crucial to note how such legendary discourses are regurgitated endlessly by university authorities to reject and repudiate protesting students. In a recent publication, Dr Dorothy Njeuma and her colleagues charge that:

> Constructive dialogue with students is rare. Students' unions created to provide a forum for negotiation with students have become a mechanism for violent confrontation rather than *dialogue, as the unions are influenced by politicians to destabilise the universities in the effort to promote particular political agendas* (Njeuma et al 1999:16 emphasis mine).

Similar accusations were made against student movements in the 1970s and 80s. In particular, they were accused of being manipulated by communist organs and international communism (Mbembe 1985:108). Parallel claims are made and replicated in the age of multiparty politics.

Can Student Activism be Depoliticised?

I have argued above that although student activism in the 1990s at UB tended to focus on issues of immediate concern to the student community, it also extended its breadth into the domains of local and national politics. It is probable that the administration's claim that students were being manipulated by politicians for alternative ends stems from students' oppositional stance with regard to issues of broader concern in the country. It should be pointed out that the increase in student activism on the African continent could be directly linked to political liberalization in the early 1990s. In Cameroon for example, 'political liberalization allowed space for students to voice their long-standing grievances about the deteriorating living and study conditions' (Konings 2002:180) while in Kenya, limited political liberalization in 1991 'reinvigorated a tradition of student activism' (Klopp and Orina 2002:46). Similar claims could be made for Nigeria where the struggle for democracy was championed by academics in collaboration with students despite stiff resistance from successive military regimes (Jega 1994). It is evident from the foregoing discussion that one cannot dissociate student activism from broader political processes, although most African governments have often sought to do so, albeit ambivalently. In Cameroon, President Paul Biya has often discouraged university students from participating in politics – '*la politique aux politiciens, l'école aux écoliers*' (cf. Konings 2002:190) but at the same time, his government has encouraged the formation of youth branches of the ruling party on campuses, particularly during the early 1990s at the University of Yaounde. The government also encouraged the formation of ethnic militia among student groups at the University of Yaounde in order to combat popular demands for democracy and political reform (cf. Konings 2002; Jua 2003; Fokwang 2003). Thus, it is unfathomable to talk of depoliticising student activism when student activism itself, by its very essence, is political. One could extend this discussion to interrogate what constitutes 'the political', not from the perspective of university administrators or researchers' agendas, but from the vantage point of the student activists themselves (cf. O'toole et al 2003).

During the student protests at Buea in the mid-1990s, one observes that broader political concerns of that era became embroiled in the crisis. At issue was the ethnicization of the student protests by indigenous groups and some members of the private press. The University of Buea is not only located in Bakweri territory, but it is also headed by members of the Bakweri ethnic group, although a majority of the students and lecturers are from the North West Province (Konings 2003:39). Despite this, there is popular talk of north western hegemony over local ethnic citizens thus pitting the latter against the former. It was along these lines that the UBSU-led protests against the authorities in November 1995 were re-interpreted by certain individuals. This became apparent at the Buea local market where 'strangers' were purportedly chased away and accused of having burnt the registrar's car.[20] Accusations were also made against prominent members of the UB administration, particularly those of North West origin for trying to undermine the vice-chancellor's legitimacy and thereby helping to fuel the protests. A columnist in a local private paper summarised the conflict in the following words:

> Too many people of the North West and possibly Manyu are simply not comfortable with having two Bakweris among the twenty-two senior officials of the University of Buea. Truth of the matter is that the Bakweris have been marginalised since reunification in 1961. The reasons, as we all know, are not far-fetched. Each time a Bakweri was earmarked for high political or administrative office, there was always the tendency to remind the powers that be of their tainted and questionable loyalty to the fatherland. Is it wrong for President Biya to have discovered merits in two Bakweris who are already creating sensation in the running of this University? Is it also wrong for a caring President to seek to right the wrongs of yester years against a humane, civilised, and liberal minded people? The North-West students and their cohorts must be told unequivocally that they cannot eat their cake and have it, and that what is good for the goose is good for the gander.[21]

While there is no evidence that student politics at UB was ethnicised as analysed in the case of the University of Yaounde by Konings (2002), it is apparent that the student protests were interpreted along the autochthony-allochthony discourses that have bedevilled Cameroon since the introduction of political liberalisation in the early 1990s. In summary, the autochthony-allochthony conflict in Cameroon and other parts of Africa has come to represent the claims of indigenous ethnic citizens against domination by so-called ethnic strangers (cf. Geschiere & Nyamnjoh 2000; Konings 2001; Bayart et al 2001). In the anglophone South West Province of Cameroon, local elites and politicians have fuelled these discourses for political gain by depicting their anglophone counterparts of the North West as dominating and exploitative (see Konings 2003 for ramifications of these discourses in recent religious conflicts in the South West Province). The fact that student politics despite itself has been interpreted along prevailing political concerns is an indication of the continuous intersection between the constituency of student activism and socio-political developments within the body politic. Thus, one cannot talk of the depoliticization of student activism as such, but rather, advocate its analysis, which by every indication can shed light on local politics.

Conclusion

This chapter has presented a detailed analysis of student activism at the University of Buea from its inception in 1993 to 2003. The above account sheds light not only on students' claims but also on the social, economic and political developments that took place during the era under consideration. I have demonstrated that one can establish a divergence between the character of student activism in the mid-1990s and its later manifestations since 1999. Between 1993 and 1996, student complaints were directed at the university authorities and when space was not provided for the articulation of their plight, activists tended to organise protests against the university administration. These protests seemed persistent despite the employment of ruthless disciplinary techniques by the administration to police students and their activities. This eventually culminated in the complete suspension of students' union politics on campus and it was only re-introduced four years later. Since 1999, student activism has been relatively less confrontational towards the university administration and directed more at civil authorities. I argued that while the university authorities might have succeeded in producing docile bodies out of the new generation of student activists, the reality is in the generational and experiential gap between activists of the early 1990s and those that took over student politics at the end of the decade. The socio-political climate has also changed, compared to the stringent economic crisis and the unstable political conditions of the early 1990s. Most of the pioneer students who enrolled at the University of Buea were formerly students at the University of Yaounde where student groups had already built a solid reputation in their clamour for political liberalisation and democracy in the country. This spirit of activism was carried along to Buea where student activists frequently confronted the administration over issues of concern to the student community.

Despite these differences, both the student protests of the early and mid-1990s as well as the recent protests in 2003 have something in common – the disposition for violence. The fact that student protests have often turned violent has created a perception of youths and students in particular as a menace to the sanity and stability of society. That notwithstanding, I argued that it is crucial to go beyond the sensational conclusions and explore the dynamics of violent protests sociologically. In this regard, I contend that violent protests could be understood not only as a form of expressing disillusionment, but also as a mode of deconstructing the postcolonial state and the legitimacy of its local auxiliaries such as government-appointed vice-chancellors and university administrators. That is to say, violent protest is not always orchestrated for its own sake, but is usually accompanied by discourses, even if such discourses are incoherent and unconvincing. Furthermore, violent protests could be responses to the symbolic and physical violence of the state against unarmed and powerless citizens.

Drawing on ethnographic data, this chapter also explored the relationship between student activism and local politics in an attempt to evaluate if student activism can be depoliticised. The chapter concludes that student politics cannot be depoliticised. In fact, it observed that an in-depth analysis of student activism can shed tremendous light on critical socio-political developments at the local and national levels.

While peaceful protest is recognised as healthy for a democracy and is 'increasingly enjoying greater legitimacy not only among government elites but also by public opinion' in several Western countries (Aelst & Walgrave 2001:480) it is unlikely that African governments would embrace this consensus for a long time to come. The integration of many African universities in the 'wider system of repressive rule' implies that the striving for 'university autonomy and academic freedom is tied to broader struggles for democracy and human rights' (Klopp & Orina 2002:45-46). For many optimistic scholars, such as Klopp & Orina, the university remains an offsetting for 'resistance and advocacy for democratic change'. Such optimism notwithstanding, the trend in Cameroonian universities is deeply distressing owing to complacency among students and faculty. Widespread corruption in the mismanagement of student funds and administrative lethargy in bringing such union leaders to justice are indications of a decaying system. However, the recent strikes that beset three of the six state universities in 2005 indicate that student activism often has serious consequences for local and national politics, hence the intertwinement between student activism and politics.

Notes

1. Christopher Ambe Shu, 'Irate varsity students stone governor over insecurity', *The Herald,* No. 1311 of 5-6 February 2003, pp. 1-2.
2. Christopher Ambe Shu, 'Police brutalize UB students for barricading road to protest insecurity', Online edition of *The Herald.* Available online at http://www.heraldnewspaper.org, January 20 2004 accessed on January 23 2004. Once again, students were expressing their disgruntlement at police negligence in dealing with calls for urgent intervention against armed burglary.

3. The four university centres were as follows: the Buea University Centre (specialising in languages, translation, interpretation and the arts); Douala University Centre for Business studies and the training of technical teachers; Dschang University Centre for Agricultural Sciences and lastly; Ngaoundere University Centre for Food Science and Food Technology (Njeuma et al 1999:5).
4. See *The Chariot,* Vol. 07, No. 3, 3.
5. The devaluation of the CFA Franc in Francophone West Africa provoked a series of strikes in some countries such as Mali and Senegal. Students played a leading role in these strikes but in Cameroon, no protest marches were organised. See Wise (1998) for an account of the student protests against the devaluation of the CFA Franc in other West African countries.
6. The ghost town operation entailed a period of civil disobedience during which cities were deserted and/or economic activities stopped. During the ghost town period, business activities were limited to Saturdays and Sundays, which permitted people to buy groceries needed for the rest of the week. The principal aim of the ghost town was to weaken the economy and force Paul Biya to resign or enter into dialogue with those advocating more democratic reform.
7. See interview with Dr Dorothy Njeuma, *The Messenger,* Vol. 1 No. 018 of Friday August 27, 1993, pp. 8-9.
8. 'Buea University Students on Strike' in *The Messenger* Vol. 1 No. 018 of Friday 27 August, 1993, 1, 8-9. The article also carries an interview with Dr Dorothy Njeuma where she presents arguments for the need to increase tuition, owing to the poor fiscal standing of the university.
9. See details of these claims by Dr Njeuma and Prof. Chumbow (then deputy vice-chancellor, now rector of the University of Yaounde 1) in *The Herald* No. 054, Wednesday September 1-8, 1993, p. 3.
10. Quoted from *The Herald* No. 055, Wednesday September 8-15, 1993, p. 8.
11. See *The Messenger* Vol. 1, No. 020, Wednesday September 22, 1993, p. 8.
12. See *The Messenger,* No. 026, Thursday November 4, 1993, p. 7.
13. Luma Slim Davis, 'Registrar Prevents Strike at University of Buea', in *The Messenger,* Vol. III, No. 036, Wednesday November 10, 1993, p. 9.
14. Peterkins Manyong, 'Distressed Buea Varsity Students cry out against Victimisation' in *The Herald,* No. 227, Thursday August 3-6, 1995, p. 2.
15. For instance, the students argued that they had been isolated from participating in preparatory meetings against the official opening of the new academic year scheduled for 30 November 1995.
16. 'University of Buea in state of emergency', *The Herald,* No. 262, Monday November 27-29, 1995, pp. 1-2.
17. See *The Herald,* No. 265, Thursday December 7-11, 1995, p. 3.
18. President Paul Biya came to power in November 1982 and has remained in power until today. He has employed various forms of 'divide and rule' especially during the multiparty era in order to resist defeat (see Eyoh 1998; Geschiere and Nyamnjoh 2000 and Takougang 2003).

19. In 2000, religious personalities, local human rights groups and Amnesty International accused the Cameroon government of carrying out extrajudicial killings. Mass graves were discovered in the outskirts of Douala provoking widespread horror among citizens, thus confirming the government's repeated denial that the accusations had been unfounded. See http://www.amnesty.org, AI INDEX: AFR 17/005/2000 4 December 2000.
20. Bekong Fondong, 'University of Buea Crisis: Bakweris attack "strangers" for burning Registrar's car', *The Herald*, No. 262, Monday November 27-29, 1995, p. 2.
21. Mohammed Molua Gbadago, 'Genesis of the Buea University Fracas' *The Star Headlines*, Vol. 5, No. 31, Monday January 15, 1996, pp. 4-5.

References

Aelst, P.V. and Walgrave, S., 2001, Who is That (Wo)man in the Street? From the Normalisation of Protest to the Normalisation of the Protester, *European Journal of Political Research*, Vol. 39, pp. 461-486.

Apter, D., 1997, 'Political Violence in Analytical Perspective', in *The Legitimization of Violence*, D. Apter (ed.), London: Macmillan Press Ltd, pp. 1-32.

Bayart, J.-F., Geschiere, P. and Nyamnjoh, F. B., 2001, *Autochtonie, démocratie et citoyenneté en Afrique. Critique Internationale*, Vol. 10, pp. 177-194.

Comaroff, J. and Comaroff, J. L., 2001, 'Reflections on Youth, From the Past to the Postcolony,' SSRC Working paper, New York.

Cruise O'Brien, D., 1996, 'A Lost Generation? Youth Identity and State Decay in West Africa', in R. Werbner and T. Ranger, eds., *Postcolonial Identities in Africa*. London: Zed Books.

Diouf, M., 2003, 'Engaging Postcolonial Cultures: African Youth and Public Space', *African Studies Review*, Vol. 46, pp. 1-12.

Dreyfus, H., L. and Rabinow, P., 1983, *Michel Foucault, Beyond Structuralism and Hermeneutics*, (2nd ed.), Chicago: University of Chicago Press.

Durham, D., 2000, 'Youth and the Social Imagination in Africa: Introduction to Parts 1 and 2", *Anthropological Quarterly*, Vol. 73, pp. 113-120.

Eyoh, D., 1998, Through the Prism of a Local Tragedy: Political Liberalization, Regionalism and Elite Struggles for Power in Cameroon, *Africa* Vol. 68, pp. 338-359.

Fokwang, J., 2003, Ambiguous Transitions: Mediating Citizenship among Youth in Cameroon', *Africa Development*, Vol. XXVIII, pp. 76–104.

Geschiere, P. and Nyamnjoh, F. B., 2000, 'Capitalism and Autochthony: The Seesaw of Mobility and Belonging', *Public Culture*, 12 pp. 423-452.

Jega, A. M., 1994, *Nigerian Academics Under Military Rule* (No. 1994, p. 3). Stockholm: University of Stockholm, Department of Political Science.

Klopp, J. M., and Orina, J. R., 2002, University Crisis, Student Activism, and Contemporary Struggle for Democracy in Kenya', *African Studies Review*, Vol. 45, pp. 43-76.

Konings, P., 2002, University Students' Revolt, Ethnic Militia, and Violence During Political Liberalization in Cameroon', *African Studies Review*, Vol. 45, p. 179.

Konings, P., 2003, 'Anglophone University Students and Anglophone Nationalist Struggles in Cameroon', Available online at http://asc.leidenuniv.nl/pdf/conference24042003-konings.pdf.

Konings, P., 2003, Religious Revival in the Roman Catholic Church and the Autochthony-Allochthony Conflict in Cameroon', *Africa*, Vol. 73, pp. 31-56.

Mashayekhi, M., 2001, 'The Revival of the Student Movement in Post-revolutionary Iran', *International Journal of Politics, Culture and Society*, Vol. 15, pp. 283-314.
Mbembe, A., 1985, *Les Jeunes et L'Ordre Politique en Afrique Noire*, Paris: L'Harmattan.
Mbembe, A., 1992, 'Provisional Notes on the Postcolony', *Africa*, Vol. 62, pp. 3-36.
Mbembe, A., 2001, *On the Postcolony*. Berkeley and Los Angeles: University of Carlifornia Press.
Naidoo, K., 1992, 'The Politics of Youth Resistance in the 1980s: The Dilemmas of a Differentiated Durban', *Journal of Southern African Studies*, Vol. 18, pp.143-165.
Njeuma, D., Endeley, H., Mbuntum, F., Lyonga, N., Nkweteyim, D., Musenja, S., and Ekanje, E., 1999, *Reforming a National System of Higher Education: The Case of Cameroon*, ADEA Working Group on Higher Education, The World Bank.
Nyamnjoh, F. B., ed., 1996, *The Cameroon G.C.E. Crisis: a test of Anglophone solidarity*, Limbe, Cameroon: Nooremac Press.
Nyamnjoh, F. B. and Jua, N., 2002, 'African Universities in Crisis and the Promotion of a Democratic Culture: The Political Economy of Violence in African Educational Systems', *African Studies Review*, Vol. 45, pp. 1-26.
O'toole, T., Lister, M., Marsh, D., Jones, S., and McDonagh, A., 2003, 'Tuning out or Left out? Participation and Non-participation Among Young People', *Contemporary Politics*, Vol. 9, pp. 46-61.
Schmidt-Soltau, K., 1999, *Living on the Edge of a Volcano - The Eruption of Democracy and Its Dnemies*, Douala: Telcam Press.
Takougang, J., 2003, 'Nationalism, Democratisation and Political Opportunism in Cameroon', *Journal of Contemporary African Studies*, Vol. 21, pp. 427-445.
Wise, C., 1998, 'Chronicle of a Student Strike in Africa: The Case of Burkina Faso', 1996-1997, *African Studies Review*, Vol. 41, pp. 19-36.

2. South Africa

Post-Apartheid Higher Education: The Role and Challenges Facing Student Activists

Mlungisi Cele

Introduction and Background

South Africa celebrates ten years of democracy this year.[1] Over this period, South African higher education (HE) institutions have witnessed a transformation of institutional governance structures and a change in patterns of student activism from active opposition to governance structures to participation, despite the fact that much of the harsh realities of the pre-1994 Apartheid landscape remain. The change in student activism from direct confrontation to engagement has been widely explained as relating to the tough positions institutions took during the mid-1990s when student demonstrations were viewed as 'not constructive' and to generational factors such as different aspirations and apathy. This paper argues that the change in governance processes and change in patterns of student activism are related, and that organizational changes in the way student bodies operate and see their role are responsible for the focus on participation and engagement. Based on interviews with current student leaders, we also show that students adapted their organizational structures to the post-1994 institutional and national political contexts and that participation in governance structures at HE institutions have produced few positive outcomes for students.

Starting with an overview of the political and ideological role students played in addressing national problems in South Africa before 1994, we examine the nature of student participation and its outcomes since 1994 by looking at the emergence of new institutional governance structures that specifically provided for student input into institutional decisions. The paper shows that there has been a considerable focus at HE institutions on increasing the supply of students and in promoting responsiveness to economic demand factors. At the same time, the central role of student politicians as architects of social change at higher education institutions has diminished with 'market' factors being blamed for educational sorting and the expulsion of large numbers of students who gained access because of increased supply, but who lack the resources to succeed.

Since most HE institutions also do not have the resources to address student demands for cheaper and more skill-intensive education and to achieve high pass rates, while responding to expansion in student numbers, we further argue that the failure to deliver outcomes, desired by student organizations through participation in governance structures, invariably means that student bodies today again face a choice with respect to their role at universities. What is important about this choice, between merely participating in structures and fighting to achieve specific outcomes, is that it reflects a tussle in student ranks about the political role they could be playing in South Africa. Looking at the relationship between university management and student organizations and how students have taken up struggles around tuition costs and financial support, we conclude by setting forth propositions about the way in which the relationship between students and university managers is likely to develop.

Part of our concern relates to how students have altered their organizational responses to the institutional problems they continue to face at universities and technikons. National retention data shows that 20-25 per cent of students continue to drop out each year. What is significant about this per centage is that it includes large numbers of students who were excluded because they could not pay their fees. For this reason, the major concern of many students is not whether they will be accepted at HE institutions, but whether they will be able to pay the costs. What is further significant about this is that student debt has crippled effective governance and offering of quality academic programmes at many institutions.

But, while student numbers, tuition fees and student debt have risen steadily over several years because subsidy funding from government has declined in real terms, and while student organizations have annually protested against exclusions and tuition increases, student organizations have on a few occasions won significant battles at universities over the last ten years in regard to exclusion, rising tuition fees and the increasing level of indebtedness. For instance, on one occasion, university authorities conceded to a judicial commission and re-registration of large numbers of excluded students after student leaders withdrew from negotiations with institutional leaders, following the death of a student in unrest-related activity in 2000 at the University of Durban Westville, and after the national Department of Education negotiated a truce that allowed for re-registration and the deferral of debt payment.

But while large numbers of students (graduates and dropouts) exit annually with huge debt at other institutions, before and after the victory at the University of Durban-Westville, organizational defenses against indebtedness have invariably involved student leaders backing down from earlier demands for re-registration of financially excluded students and participating in decisions on who should be allowed back and on the payment conditions tied to re-registration. These decisions have generally taken the form of agreeing that students who passed their courses, but owe money, should be accommodated if their debt falls in a certain range, while those who struggle academically should be excluded. This pattern of participating in executive decisions and providing legitimacy to decisions that exclude probably 10-15 per cent of students annually can be observed at almost all higher education institutions since 1994.

At most institutions, the trend has involved initial student rejection of exclusions, protest against exclusions and then acceptance of exclusions following managerial efforts to first 'bully' student leaders through police involvement and then, through consultation, to win them over, and bind their future actions to support the exclusion of poor students from working class and rural communities. This response from student leaders stands in stark contrast to earlier times when student leaders and organizations resorted to more violent actions to highlight their grievances and to pressurize university managers. For example, for much of the 1980s and early to mid-1990s, student actions ranged from marches, to sit-ins, hostage-taking, vandalism, pickets, placard demonstrations, boycotts and disruption of administrative activities when faced with problems.

For us, this presents an intriguing puzzle. Considering that lengthy institutional protests generally resulted in HE authorities addressing and conceding to student demands to avoid lengthy and damaging image battles, we are interested in establishing why the change in student responses occurred and what students have achieved through participation in governance structures. We are also interested in establishing how students have defined their role in post-Apartheid South Africa and their contribution towards enhancing, consolidating and deepening democracy as active citizens both within and outside campuses. Further, we are interested in establishing how student leaders and university managers negotiate the 'response options' they face when addressing discontent that has variously focused on rising tuition fees (that even middle-class households struggle with), overcrowding in residences and lecture rooms, accusations that institutions develop at too slow pace, accusations about racist and discriminatory behaviour, concern about pass rates and so on and so forth. In this regard, our interest lies in reasons for a single-track approach to 'student problems' versus reasons why students have not used complimentary strategies.

It is particularly clear that student leaders, on the one hand, are caught between the traditional resistance and oppositional politics that characterized the pre-1994 period, and the consequences of their participation – rather than rejection – of institutional governance structures that make them jointly responsible for policy issues that shape educational outcomes for other students. In terms of the first approach, it is a familiar tactic to different student generations and has a 'track record' that students fall back on. Traditionally, its success also provided a yardstick to measure the organizational muscle of student leaders. For this, and for other reasons, traditional protest actions, whether organized or spontaneous, in the past often emerged as the first method through which student frustration was expressed. These methods also continue to be widely used, as witnessed by the fact that organized and spontaneous protests involving marches and pickets occurred at almost all HE institutions over the past three years.

But, what also stands out in the present context is the strong negative reaction that such actions have elicited in the press, from government, and at institutions where fellow students and executive managers have strongly condemned protest. What is further instructive about the continuing reliance on these tactics is that organized demonstrations, over the last three years have mainly involved passive tactics and have generally not threatened academic or administrative functioning, while spontaneous actions have achieved the opposite.

What has, however, also happened is that the second approach has increasingly gained currency. For most of the early 1990s, this happened as a consequence of student leaders relying on discussions with managers to have vandalism and criminal intent charges dropped. But, the second approach is also largely a consequence of the negotiated settlement that led to the birth of the post-1994 democracy in South Africa, and renewed interest in this country in negotiations as a means of resolving resource inequalities. Before 1994, student leaders often refused to recognize management structures at universities and technikons and at times adopted a policy of non-collaboration that included not participating in institutional functions such as graduations. This policy was linked to social, political, economic and institutional realities that especially limited student autonomy at historically black higher education institutions in South Africa. While negotiation later provided a successful model for national political change our puzzle is why students follow this model and its associated trappings of participation in governance structures when the participation rules are strongly weighted against students acquiring any significant say in any policy issue that they collectively address with academics and university and technikon managers.

Data and Structure

This paper is largely conceptualized as a comment on the role of students in South African society. In preparing it, we draw together a broad range of sociological arguments on the role of students. We relate these arguments to case study data on how student leaders view the outcomes of their participation in governance structures. Regarding this, the empirical information on which this paper is based derives from data collected from students and Student Representative Council

(SRC) members at 20 institutions. This includes a survey questionnaire administered to 467 students at University of Durban-Westville (UDW) and Western Cape (UWC). This discussion focuses on the consequences of their involvement in institutional governance.

In addressing the role of students and the organizational challenges they face, this paper is divided into four sections. Section one situates our analysis within a broader socio-economic and political context. This is underlined by at least three sets of the underlying assumptions with related questions. That is, post-apartheid higher education transformation cannot be conceived in isolation from the reconstruction and development process of SA. In this regard, we need to ask the question: how can the relation between higher education transformation and reconstruction and development be conceptualized as integral and yet limitations of higher education transformation still be exposed? To what extent does this impact on the way students engage in the role they are supposed to be playing? This particularly poses a challenge to SASCO which is biggest national student organization and has a strategic and organic relationship with the ANC.

Second, student movement strategy should be understood in relation to the conditions which are internal and external to it. Thus, does raising questions about whether the composition, organization and leadership of students determine student approaches and strategies or the 'objective pre-suppositions' play any role and, if so, how are we to understand that role? Third, it is crucial to determine and analyse the effect, not only of the form of state, but also of the structure of the political terrain on the student organizational and strategic possibilities in a particular period.

Section three provides a lens through which to examine the role of students in South Africa in the post-apartheid transformation and the difficulties student organizations face in organizing support and protest. Many students at higher education institutions are members of a transitional generation whose early childhood was bound to Apartheid and political repression. But their post-Apartheid experiences are in many ways characterized by signs of increased social mobility, educational opportunities, rampant consumerism, high unemployment and new forms of youth culture that for some emphasize a 'free at last' syndrome that leads to pursuit of social pleasures. For example, segments of black youth are widely described as forming part of 'Kwaito' and 'Jam Alley' – referring to a popular local music genre and TV programme that promote black youth as sexually involved and free-spending generations.

Section four profiles the composition of the student body in order to better understand the students we discuss. What is important about the students we profile is that many are beneficiaries of the student demand for increased access to university and technikon education. We show that this has produced increased diversity in student ranks, but has also meant that a wide gap exists between those who should have been there and those who gained access through politics. But while many students have gained access through political factors we point out that this has not necessarily added political weight to the activities of student organizations. Most incoming students today are women who also take extra classes to address academic development gaps, enroll in non-Humanities fields, and reject politics, because it affects educational and occupational outcomes.

Section five examines their organizational responses since 1994 and shows that much of the post-apartheid reorganization in higher education has involved an explicit focus on process and stability issues, and not on equitable outcomes. We show that student organizations have contributed to stabilizing higher education because the dominant student organization, the South African Student Congress (SASCO),[2] saw its role as both 'complimentary and confrontational', meaning that it helped to strengthen initiatives aimed at implementing and defending or challenging the educational policies of the ruling government and its transformation process. However, this student organization has not managed to strike a sufficient balance between the objectives. Finally, we argue that educational sorting has meant that the prime beneficiaries of increased student access are also the prime losers because the level of investment into HE institutions has made high dropout rates inevitable and raises important questions about the future strategies students could use to influence outcomes more positively for their peers.

Socio-economic and Political Context of the Post-1994 South Africa

Rather than conducting a comprehensive analysis of the post-1994 South African situation, we simply highlight a set of conditions that could potentially structure and influence the role and challenges facing students while recognizing the dynamic character of students as agents of change. South Africa's transition to democracy came as a result of a negotiated settlement. For the ANC, as it stood in 1997, neither the democratic movement nor the apartheid regime had emerged as an outright victor at the beginning of the negotiations.[3]

The dynamics of the negotiation process had the effect of politically marginalizing previously important social groups such as black students and youth (Badat, Barends, Wolpe 1995:13; see also SASCO Political Report 1996). Students became spectators and were glued to television in order to keep abreast of new developments or outcomes of the negotiation process, to such an extent that the effect of this is still manifest in the student movement, particularly its inability to clearly identify a role for itself in the post-apartheid transformation.

Contrary to a widely held liberal view, South Africa's negotiated settlement was neither a miracle nor exceptional. Instead, it was a consequence of many factors including the sacrifices, long protracted struggles of the downtrodden which spanned over three centuries. Its unique feature is that it took place against the backdrop of the dissolution of the Soviet bloc of countries under one superpower, the Soviet Union, at the end of Cold of War. However, this did not mean, as Nzimande (2003), cautioned a freer and conflict-free world, as the advocates of benign globalization and 'end of history' ideologues would want us to believe. South Africa's negotiated transition shares commonalities with transitions in developing countries (Africa, Latin America and Asia) in the 1980s. For instance, these transitions were accompanied by low-intensity conflicts, warfare and attempts by the old ruling bloc to exploit differences among oppressed people (ethnic, religious, language, class, gender and racial contradictions) to fragment and weaken the democratic and oppressed forces so as to produce of a particular kind of product.

The apartheid regime particularly intensified its low-conflict warfare, promoted violence and attempted to create hatred of the democratic movement among the oppressed themselves (Nzimande 2003). The democratic movement foiled these attempts, but a tone for compromises had already been set regarding the establishment of a government of national unity, the entrenchment of some of the rights of the existing public service, including the security forces, the judiciary and para-statals, and the establishment of provinces with original powers. This meant that the democratic movement inherited the apartheid state machinery that was intact, orderly within its own rules, and with the majority resolved to continue in their positions and any attempt to transform these would have met with resistance from within. For Nzimande, the democratic movement did not in its theory, strategies and conceptions of democratic South Africa plan for these compromises which profoundly conditioned the character of the reconstruction process, including education.

South Africa's negotiated transition involved a compromise and trade-off between inclusive political democracy, while leaving the economic structure intact (Nzimande 2003). This resulted in a democracy with political power but no economic power. The fact that the transition was negotiated was not a consequence of an overthrow of the apartheid regime reflected the prevailing balance of class power, and implied recognition of white's inclusion in the social structure and their property rights (Gelb 2005: 368). Such business demands helped to frame the negotiation process and a resumption of capital inflows was one of the top priorities. On the other hand, there were social and political imperatives to reverse racial discrimination in the distribution of wealth, income and goods and services in both public and private sectors.

According to Gelb (2005:369) the top priority in deracializing economic power was 'capital reform' (equivalent to land reform), or opening the ownership and management of private corporations and the direction of state institutions and public corporations to the black middle classes, obtaining access to power, influence and remuneration. The negotiated nature of the transition meant that capital reform would necessarily be an incremental, market-focused process engaging with current owners of capital. A second imperative was the reallocation of public expenditure on goods and services to reflect the racial composition of the popular, to address social exclusion and poverty.

Some of the landmarks of the negotiated transition include the adoption of the Interim Constitution, the 1994 elections, the very act of dislodging the apartheid regime from power, the establishment and adoption of the Constitution with a single South African citizenship and which was based on the principles of democracy, non-sexism and non-racialism, the abolition of both the tricameral and Bantustan systems and legislating equality before the law including gender equality. These could be seen as contributing towards addressing the national question and in laying the basis for nation-building and reconciliation, cornerstones of the reconstruction of society.

During the first decade of freedom, the democratic state put strong emphasis on nation-building and reconciliation — an imperative of stabilizing democracy with numerous consequences. For example, the working class and poor had to abandon or retreat from struggling for their own demands while at the same time both local and global capital forces including elements within the democratic movement took advantage of and exploited a space by playing a dominant role in shaping and influencing the new state regarding economic restructuring. At the same time, SACP (2005) argued that nation-building, reconciliation and the imperative of stabilizing democracy served as a shield behind which global and domestic capital forces began to advance and consolidate their class interests and agenda and to forge an elite pact — a class compromise which required an offensive against the working class, the poor, and the public sector.

This has involved both attempts at major restructuring of the economy, including the labour market — mass retrenchments, casualisation, informalisation, privatisation, and the fragmentation of the public and parastatal sector (see also Desai and Pithouse 2004: 845). In this regard, it is women who have borne the brunt of retrenchments and casualization in two ways: firstly, as direct victims, but secondly, as the ones who normally have to face and deal with the reality of poverty in the household. However, it would be wrong to project women primarily as victims. Millions of working class and poor women have been and continue to be involved in the liberation struggle (SACP 200; see also Daniel and Habib 2003; Terreblanche 2004; Desai 2003).

The current South Africa's socio-economic trajectory is contradictory. It is acknowledged that if the 'dynamic of inclusion and exclusion' continues along the same trajectory, it will pose a major threat to our democracy as it enters its second decade of freedom — especially if the 'negatives' overwhelm the 'positives'.[4] On the one hand, there is a systemic persistence of poverty, unemployment and underemployment — a point that has been underlined by various research projects, including that which informed the government's recent ten-year self-review. According to Bond (2004), unemployment rose from 16 per cent in 1995 to 30 per cent in 2002. Adding frustrated job seekers to that figure brings the total unemployed to 43 per cent. Youth unemployment stood at 47 per cent. Worsening poverty and rising water and electricity prices together accounted for 30 per cent of the income of those earning less than R500 per month: ten million people had their water disconnected, according to national government surveys, and ten million were also victims of electricity disconnections (see also Desai 2002; Terreblanche 2003; Desai and Pithouse 2004).

In addition, according to Bond (2004), a government agency, Statistics South Africa, released a report in October 2002 confirming that in real terms, the average black "African" household income declined by 19 per cent from 1995 to 2000, while white household income rose by 15 per cent. The average black household earned one-sixth as much the average white household in 2000, down from a quarter in 1995. Households with less than R670 per month income (mainly black African, coloured and of Asian descent) increased from 20 per cent of the population in 1995 to 28 per cent in 2000. Across the racial divides, the poorest half of all South Africans earned just 9.7 per cent of national income, down from 11.4 per cent in 1995. The richest 20 per cent earned 65 per cent of all income (Statistics South Africa, Earning and Spending in South Africa (Pretoria: Statistics South Africa 2002; Business Day 2002 November 22).

On the other hand, in 2004, the country achieved macroeconomic stability, which was firmly entrenched with the fiscal deficit being consistently low, inflation was within the 3-6 per cent target range, net foreign reserves stood at R11.4 billion up from minus R25 billion in 1994; and the prime overdraft was down from 25.5 per cent in 1994 to 11 per cent. The economy grew at an estimated rate of 3.8 per cent in 2004, forecasted at 4 per cent for 2005. Investment by government and the private sector improved from 14 per cent to 16 per cent. In mid-2005, business confidence was said to be at an all time high.

The current socio-economic situation is characterised by shifts from the Reconstruction Development Programme (RDP) to Growth, Employment and Redistribution (GEAR) to the post-2002 anti-privatisation era of 'developmental and interventionist change'. Whereas there is no consensus as to whether three policies represent a shift or not, there is no doubt, though that they (especially GEAR) have been a site of struggle and the object of resentment especially from the working class and poor and student movement who blamed it for the current social inequalities. GEAR was imposed and cast as 'non-negotiable' and promised, among other things, to create about 400,000 jobs by the year 2000 – which obviously did not happen. It has been described as a voluntary structural programme. Although the realisation that getting economic fundamentals right will not on its own eradicate social inequalities, at least the early obsession with this objective is beginning to make way for a broader and all-encompassing approach which government seems to be taking. However, the key question is to what extent is this shift to developmental and interventionist policies a sustainable and effective means to address dynamics of inclusion and exclusion and all forms of social inequalities.

Perspectives on the Role of Students and HE Institutions

There is a voluminous body of international research on the political role of students in developed and underdeveloped countries. Most of this writing draws on the distribution of power and social control in a particular country and argues that universities by virtue of their special role in maturation provide students with an important site in which to engage in transformative activism and in which to foster democratic civic notions. In these perspectives, students are not viewed as merely passive receptors of information, but as individuals who contribute to society's development through active involvement, despite the wide acknowledgement that while some parts of higher education are devoted to producing knowledgeable well rounded individuals, others are equally concerned with producing narrow trades' people.

University education is further viewed as an opportunity for students to use their status, knowledge and sense of freedom to engage in diverse activities and to critically address pressing university and societal problems. It also affords them space for the emergence of radical and militant leaders. Among these latter students, a small number, who act as 'shock troopers', provide leadership through democratically elected or ad-hoc voluntary structures and use methods that range from street protest to negotiation and abstention to highlight their views and to influence others. However, the majority who remain politically inactive, typically adapt to the institutions' dominant system of values and norms, do not 'rock the boat', and act consistent with their end goals of graduating and using HE as a social mobility mechanism. For most students, this goal is consistent with their aspirations of benefiting from HE by getting a good job, starting a family and enjoying consumerism.

In so far as these research results have been applied to South African students, there has generally been agreement that HE, with some exceptions, continues to be for the elite. Thus, even among Coloureds and Africans, who on average are the poorest in South Africa, and among whom the middle class group is still relatively underdeveloped, it is clear that most university graduates come from areas where home-ownership has become the norm. It is also obvious that while there are many examples of poor students from working-class and rural communities succeeding at universities and technikons, it is equally true that many of these proletarian students drop out of university and take many years to complete their education since this is often interspersed with full-time employment.

For most of these students, the main reason for dropout is their working-class status and the fact that available student funding barely covers tuition fees, and leaves most of them owing more than they paid toward their studies.

However, while all the students view HE as a key to opportunities that will improve their labour-market position, three basic propositions exist on the broader purpose of HE institutions and role of students in South Africa. The first perspective, which focuses on supply-side factors (and pays homage to an early student demand that the doors of learning and culture should remain open), is influenced by functionalist discourse. This argues that universities and technikons fulfil both a labour-market and welfare function by minimising unemployment and providing some skills and mobility prospects. In this view, universities and technikons are essentially sponges that take in large numbers of student at the behest of politicians and student protest groups, but fail to provide them with real opportunities for educational success and contribute to educational and labour-market problems.[5] As captured in a comment on student unrest, the main reason for the internal failure of institutions invariably relates to an inability on the part of the governing party to allocate sufficient resources to help HE institutions promote the life chances of HE recruits, due to competing investment claims.

The second perspective views HE institutions as a microcosm of the larger society and argues that the strain of transformation is fought out between contending forces within institutions with students playing a crucial role as change agents in using their knowledge to articulate views about a more just society.[6] In this view, student struggles are not about forces external to HE, but are inherent in resource scarcity within HE institutions and the relation between this and investment and allocation decisions by the governing party. In contrast to the pessimistic view of students as drains on society, this perspective further depicts students as key players in civil society who contribute positively to the development of society and help to extend notions of civic engagement and democracy by using their knowledge to improve broader life chances.

The third perspective sees HE institutions as demand-oriented in terms of serving the labour market and as providing narrow technical education that contributes to student apathy. In this perspective, students neither drain societal resources, nor do much to advance social needs. They rather act in their narrow self-interest, advance consumerism and indirectly contribute to more general wellbeing by paying taxes, but make little active commitment to developing society. On the other hand, HE institutions become more demand-and-vocation-oriented and develop new programmes, emphasize different outcomes and try to establish more links with business and industry in order to help promote economic growth.

These perspectives all emphasize the production function of HE and, in part, whether and how students contribute to society. The production feature does not however exhaust the role of HE institutions as captured in South African writings. Aside from these production functions, HE institutions have also played a vital role in addressing the 'student problem' of groups of students engaging in revolutionary actions and the political problem of ensuring that HE institutions remain academically sound and politically stable. Historically, HE institutions in South Africa, with one exception, remained true to their conservative roots, but allowed students room to 'find their feet'. Thus, especially white students, in the past, were able to use their status to advance their mobility and the claims of universities to be autonomous institutions, to sporadically protest against inequalities in South Africa because English universities, in particular, espoused liberal philosophies and academic freedom and imbued students with values of respect and fairness.

On the other hand, black students, whose university education was more tightly controlled by the Apartheid state, did the same under much harsher institutional conditions and faced more direct state reprisals, and repression, and greater resource scarcity. They also did so in contexts in which various leftwing ideologies such as liberation theology, black consciousness, Pan-Africanism and Marxism had taken root and co-existed alongside more conservative and orthodox views of economic, social and political engagement. In this sense, while HE institutions have always been connected through their leaders to the ruling government, the purpose of production activities never solely related to producing apathetic students, but rather emphasized that students, as consumers of HE services, had choices, a degree of freedom in which to exercise these choices and a responsibility to help contribute to developing the society.

However, since economic and political factors always limited black advancement, many participated in development activities and student politics, although many students also did not participate. For example, between 1960 and 1980 black students at white institutions largely refrained from political activities, while most other students at black and white institutions did not involve themselves in associational activities, despite considerable resource scarcity. Indeed, while the romantic view of student struggles during the 1970s and 1980s suggests that students acted in unison when opposing Apartheid, the reality was vastly different. While opposition to Apartheid was widespread and mostly fomented by 'professional Marxist revolutionaries' and 'nationalists' (the 'shock troopers'), who believed that student interests were harmoniously aligned and that universities were instruments of the Apartheid order, and structures that could be turned against 'their master's, this unity was often assumed.

One often-cited case that illustrates the folly of this utopian view concerns developments at the most radical anti-Apartheid university during the 1980s: the University of the Western Cape, whose Rector, reflecting the views of a significant segment of academic staff, grandly proclaimed that the institution would transform itself from the 'University of the Working Class' into 'The Intellectual Home of the Left' and become a 'People's University' dedicated to overthrowing Apartheid. In this view, students at the university were a united class whose main aim were not academic graduation, but contributing to the struggle against racial and class inequalities in South Africa. This recognized that Apartheid defined the role and contribution of students and that black students could not stand apart from their social context. Thus, student leaders and political organizations argued that black students were first members of their society and communities and secondly operated as students. Conceptually, this reduced the role of students to their social context, but obscured the connection among South African students between ethnicity and social class, financial difficulties, political involvement, field of study and a host of other variables.

But, not only do students come from different social and cultural environments and have different goals, student bodies were also often divided on the best way through which opposition should be expressed, if at all. That this should be so is not surprising. Students in South Africa attend three types of HE institutions: historically black, historically white English or historically white Afrikaans. Historically, these institutions were separated by their relations to the governing party as defined by language and in cultural and political terms. In turn, their student bodies owed different allegiances to the governing party and expressed their support or frustration against the governing party and its policies in terms of these allegiances, with students at Afrikaans universities and technikons at times venting their support for racially based policies. What this point partly underscores is the simple fact that students in South Africa were fragmented. Many also still come from different cultural and socio-economic backgrounds that have largely been left untouched by South Africa's transition.

As before, many of these students are also disillusioned with politics and express antipathy to actions that disrupt academic programmes. Various journalists and political commentators have highlighted that many students are more concerned with social bashes, finding jobs, completing their studies and paying off debt than financial difficulties of fellow students and that they show dissatisfaction with the public demonstration methods used by national political student organizations. Students have also been described as disinterested in politics, disillusioned with the manner in which protest and negotiations take place and as wanting everyday issues addressed.

Some[7] further argued that this student apathy relates to a view that student representatives cannot solve many of the day-to-day issues affecting students. Certainly, prevailing historical factors limit the likelihood that accumulated student debt can be written off, as student organizations once demanded. Nor can higher education institutions create jobs or eliminate racism. Disinterest in politics is possible because students lack confidence in their representatives, because they find past protest activities alienating and because recent key criticisms of SRC members and of members of political organizations concern the view that they are riding on the 'gravy train' and engage in corruption. Many have also been accused of being incompetent, not possessing basic organizational skills and needing leadership training.

Factors that Influence Student Behaviour

It is indeed possible that such factors have affected student interest in broad social and political activities. It is also possible that this may relate to differences in social upbringing since it is clear that black students today tend to play a more dominant role in political matters at all institutions where they have a tangible presence. Indeed, while it is beyond the scope of the present paper to comment on political socialization, it is evident that for many current black students whose early childhood was rooted in Apartheid, their educational socialization at secondary level often involved rapid movement from under-resourced schools to semi-private high schools and moving from townships to suburbs for better quality education. Along with those who are used to private education and those from schools in white areas, they now share university places with small numbers who progressed through disadvantaged schools and enjoyed less privileged education. In this regard, students for whom the character of education has remained the same since 1994, despite huge investments in post-Apartheid schooling, find themselves lumped with others whose educational and political socialization differs significantly.

What this means is that HE in South Africa now has to cater for a more diverse group of students than before and have to facilitate their adaptation to university life. But while they differ, they also show signs of accommodating new expectations. Thus, while all are exposed to the same consumer products and images directed at youth, all do not have the same economic security, or desire the same cultural artifacts, or share the same political views, background, or social orientations. But they also participate in the same youth market and having something like a common youth culture, in which there is a concerted battle for their hearts and minds and for encouraging values of individualism and the pursuit of money and material symbols.

But while their aspirations seem heavily materialistic, they also do not all face the same futures. As before, for many students the future is uncertain. There are signs of graduate unemployment in various fields, and that graduates take time to secure jobs. Many students believe that affirmative action will threaten job opportunities for them. Many wish to escape the introduction of community service that now applies to health professionals. Many are not sure whether they will complete their academic studies. Many also expect university education to include sufficient time for social activity. And, many believe that diversity needs to be promoted and that they share a common future, but also see little future in political activity, or believe that they can live off the political activity of others. In this latter view, some students believe that black students are best placed to win institutional gains and that they need not actively support particular struggles since gains apply to all.

For these reasons, the 'Kwaito' and 'Jam Alley' generations which prefer social to political activities are in many ways similar to white students who come from different social backgrounds and life experiences, but have similar educational and occupational aspirations and depend on university and technikon education for mobility. Many are also viewed as marginalized by a society that invests too little in their occupational futures and are therefore believed to be reluctant to participate in national government elections. However, because political organizations require their support, their impact on universities has also been significant. Consider the following: in 1988, the Student Representative Council (SRC) at the University of the Western Cape organized three functions for students, compared to seven organized fifteen years later by the SRC. In 1988, the functions related to 'welcoming first-year students', an end-of-term ball and an end-of-year function. In 2003, the functions included two Jazz festivals, two beauty pageants and the traditional welcome and farewell. Furthermore, in 2003 the SRC, as in previous years, made money available to a broad range of clubs for day-events, tours, balls and other social events. But whereas this shows a sharp increase in sponsored events at the University of the Western Cape, the number of events is small compared to those offered at some other institutions where student leaders openly argue that it is their job to 'entertain' their fellow students.

For this reason, several SRCs have over the last few years begun to hold their 'major bash' – to which 'youth stars' are invited because students need 'top performances' – just before the annual student elections in order to spur the future electoral chances of those who wish to return to office, or to give an impetus to the organization they represent. Several SRCs also focus exclusively on social events and argue that such events constitute the mainstay of student activity. The pulling power of such events for SRCs and student political organization is all the more obvious, given the fact that it is now customary for black student political organizations to refine their tactics in order to appeal to the "Kwaito' generation. Thus, almost all now combine political and social programmes to maintain student interest in politics and typically link a short political programme to a social event. One other area in which this has also happened is student elections in which manifesto readings have changed significantly with each candidate, at most institutions, only being offered two minutes to present reasons why they should be elected. This has directed attention from the issues students represent to popularity contests between individuals and gimmicks through which students try to grab the limelight.

But, while fewer social events took place before, and while beauty pageants were viewed as 'cattle shows' and outlawed at several universities before 1994, in many ways segments of the present generation are much the same as before, albeit in a different context. Thus, while politically minded students tackled the apartheid state before 1994, at most black universities social fragmentation and differences in the goals students desired from university education still revealed a lack of unity. For this reason, groups of politically-minded students at times using coercion and violence through the operation of 'disruption squads' to enforce class boycotts at some institutions and to ensure that the romantic notion of unified opposition to Apartheid by the oppressed was maintained. While not empirically established and while neither motives nor assumed social class behaviour are immutable, these divisions were largely attributed to differences in social standing of students with students from proletarian backgrounds often projected as pro-boycott (along with a small group of radical students from middle class backgrounds) compared to students with higher social standing who were often more interested in realizing the academic objectives of their university study and who wanted to study without interruptions to their academic programmes.

However, while pro-and anti-boycott positions as a way of highlighting collective opposition to Apartheid policies marked some differences in student ranks during the 1980s, one simple fact that most commentators, who observe student struggles, have highlighted since 1994 concerns an obvious change in the way especially students at historically black universities have responded to institutional and political student issues. In its simplest organizational form, at historically black universities, this has involved a shift away from using mass meetings, often attended by less than ten per cent of a student body who decided on student responses to institutional and national grievances on behalf of everyone, to using a broader range of decision-making measures that minimize the influence of a segment in decision-making and strategy formation. Embedded in this switch is an implicit shift from what some viewed as 'mob-rule' to more consultative, time- consuming and less confrontational engagement between students and university managers.

What is significant about this shift is that it points to a move away from pressure politics to a pre-occupation with administrative and management-related issues and places increased emphasis on the development of procedures and decision-making mechanisms to deal with a broad range of issues. What is further significant about the shift is that it constitutes a response to the view that working class kids who have working class problems at HE institutions were holding institutions and other students hostage by resorting to undemocratic 'mob-rule' procedures and that the shift allows HE institutions the opportunity to deal with the 'students problem' as a problem of a segment of students. In this way, 'student problems' become issues that do not affect the majority and do not interrupt academic programmes.

An example of this is a march of 200 students at the University of Cape Town (UCT) who demanded that arrangements should be made to allow them to register for academic studies in 2001. Asked to comment on public radio,[8] a UCT spokesperson, remarked that the students had failed to secure financial aid the previous year, but had nonetheless decided to study at UCT. As such, the march represented the actions of a small band that were responsible for their own situation and in no way indicated unhappiness with the core academic and business activities at UCT. Further, while the students' case merited empathy, it did not imply that student representatives were organizing political support on their behalf or that the institution would be affected by student activism. Instead, the incident was regrettable.

This depiction of a student response to an education-related grievance contrasts starkly with the focus of many earlier student struggles, which were about political discrimination, social injustice and economic inequality. Indeed, while education-specific grievances were not neglected, the critical role students played during the 1970s and 1980s in promoting social and political change involved consciousness-raising activities to create a groundswell of opposition to government policies and building strong civic orientations by fostering links between community organizations and students. Student activities also extended to playing a leading role in providing organizational assistance to the emerging black trade union movement during the 1970s and to providing coherence to social struggles by pointing to an ideological base for the promotion of inequality and by putting forward alternative social visions. As demonstrated by police beatings on campuses, the imprisonment of student leaders and the fear and repulsion that brutality induced, Apartheid in South Africa became the hegemonic project that glued liberal and radical and black and some white students together despite often stark differences in terms of social background, political orientation, ideology, strategy, approaches and organizational methods.

What the UCT incident, by contrast, illustrates is that the focus on reducing financial concerns of students to the 'problem' of a segment effectively demobilizes, and uses negotiations as a means to address issues often elicits concern, but also demobilizes student protesters because involvement involves following procedures to address problems. For student leaders, this model of student involvement in university affairs during the 1990s is essentially new and very much a consequence of changing times. Social context previously placed some students in opposition to the state and to university managers and gave rise to the establishment of non-inclusive decision-making bodies and abstention politics because student leaders invariably rejected separate organizational structures. However, changes in the political landscape in 1994 ushered in changes in the HE landscape involving the introduction of structures that gave students joint decision-making powers in relation to the distribution of resources.

The opening up of international opportunities to student organizations in the sporting and cultural arena and demand that universities and technikons pay greater attention to 'student affairs' and the quality of the student experience also meant that the way in which higher education authorities viewed students changed after 1994. This occurred especially at historically black institutions where the post-1994 changes have often involved calls to improve the quality of student experience in order to address the cumulative disadvantage of taking in large numbers of poorly prepared students and trying to develop them academically in a resource scarred environment. But, since these students, at many institutions, are further divided for the most part from other more affluent students by race, language and class differences it also meant that students could no longer maintain the illusion that the institutional interests and grievances of all students were aligned.

Composition of the Student Body

Much of the above touches on the question of the changing composition of the student body, and their financial status. For the most part, the demographic composition of the student body has changed significantly since 1980 and is beginning to reflect the composition of the national population. As described in the 2001 National Plan for Higher Education the most striking change in the growth of the HE student body concerns the enrolment of black students which increased from 191 000 to 343 000 between 1993 and 1999, i.e. by 152000 (or from 40 per cent to 80 per cent, and the enrolment and distribution of African students who in 1999 constituted 59 per cent of the total head count enrolments in higher education. This headcount enrolment, in 1999, compared with a national population distribution, which indicated that Africans constituted 76 per cent of the total population. Concerning their distribution,

In 1993, 49 per cent of African students were enrolled in the historically black institutions, 13per cent in the historically white institutions, and 38 per cent in the two distance education institutions. This had changed by 1999 to 23 per cent in the historically black institutions, 41per cent in historically white institutions, and 27 per cent in the distance education institutions. As this indicates there has been a shift in enrolment of African students to historically white institutions. This is a direct result of the availability of places at these institutions and a threefold increase in the number of African students at universities over the last ten years and a fourfold increase in their enrolment at technikons over this period.

More specifically, between 1993 and 1999 African student enrolments: (a) Decreased by 7 000 (or 9 per cent) in the historically black universities; (b) Increased by 22,000 (or 138 per cent) in the historically black technikons; (c) Increased by 10,000 (or 100 per cent) in the historically white English-medium universities; (d) Increased by 56,000 (or 1120 per cent) in the historically white Afrikaans-medium universities; (e) Increased by 49,000 (or 490 per cent) in the historically white technikons; (e) Increased by 22 000 (or 31 per cent) in the two dedicated distance education institutions.

What is also important about these changes in enrolment is that in the post-1994 period, as mentioned above, there was a shift away from enrolment at black universities to white universities who offered a better quality student experience, higher academic standards, greater academic and effective support, improved mobility opportunities, a more stable institutional environment, better accommodation and improved chances of finding donor support for studies.[9]

Four other points are noteworthy:

Much of the growth in black students at white Afrikaans-medium universities occurred in distance education programmes and in e-campus programmes. This implicitly means that large numbers of black students are not properly integrated into institutional affairs and lack a voice, except where representation is provided for sectional groups in institutional matters.

The increasing diversity of the national student body resulted in an increase in the number of international students from about 10,000 in 1993 to 43,000 (7 per cent of the national student body) in 2002.[10] What stands out about these students is the fact that most come from SADC countries, attend the distance education university and historically white English universities and international students constitute almost 30 per cent of doctoral candidates.

The growth in black student numbers has been accompanied by a decline in white student enrolments. This fell from 222,000 in 1993 to 164,000 in 1999 — a decline of 58,000 (or 26 per cent). In terms of total enrolments, gender equity has been achieved in the higher education system. This is a consequence of significant differences in headcount growth since 1993. Whereas female headcount enrolments increased by 89,000 (or 44 per cent) between 1993 and 1999, that is, from 202,000 to 291,000, by contrast, male headcount enrolments grew by only 2000 (or one per cent) between 1993 and 1999. The main result of these different growth rates is that the proportion of female students in the higher education system has risen from 43 per cent in 1993 to 52 per cent in 1999. However, gender equity continues to remain a problem in the technikons, where the proportion of female enrolments increased from 32 per cent to 42 per cent in 1999. Furthermore, as with black students, the spread of female students across different programme areas remains uneven with female students clustered in the humanities and under-represented in science, engineering and technology, business and commerce, and in postgraduate programmes. The majority of students (82 per cent) surveyed in the study indicated that the SRCs should promote debates on equity, gender and non-sexism on campuses.

Concerning the financial status of students, no detailed empirical data are available on income levels of parents, their educational and occupational background as well as resources they have and plans to finance their children's HE education. The result is that very little empirical information is available on social class positions although there is a broad range of indirect indicators that is suggestive and demonstrative of significant divergence in social class positions. Among these factors, 80 per cent study full-time and 20 per cent part-time, with most part-time students involved in undergraduate studies. While some of these students qualify for tertiary education due to age exemptions, most accumulate money in order to pay for their education. This is largely a consequence of their financial status.

Besides, national socio-economic data indicate sharp variance in average income levels of black and white South Africans, which largely underscores the point that race remains an indicator of social class in South Africa. Another indicator relates to debt levels of black and white students that further illustrate the difference. While the extent of this debt varies at any given moment during a financial year, student debt at historically black institutions reached R500 million at one point in 1998. Considering that this total was almost equal to the state subsidy allocated to four historically black universities in 1998, it is easy to see why student debt was responsible for huge debts owed to banks by most of these institutions in 1999 and the need for urgent government action to minimize debt levels that accumulated steadily from 1993.

That this debt is indicative of an inability to pay fees is not disputed, although it has been argued that some student leaders and student organizations, by the mid-1990s, did not accept the notion that students should share in the costs of their higher education. This latter position relates to a demand for free education, which some student leaders believed should be a policy goal of the African National Congress. Nor is it disputed that the inability to pay is largely found at historically black institutions or that probably more than 50 per cent of students at historically black institutions need loans and scholarships to afford HE. For this reason, students at these institutions were initially the main beneficiaries of loans provided to students by government through its national loan scheme (National Student Financial Aid Scheme - NSFAS) introduced in 1994. This scheme has to date supported more than 300,000 students although it does not cover all student costs. In fact, most students owe considerable amounts because the scheme allocates a minimum of about R2000 and a maximum of about R18,000 to each student, with an average of about R6000 to students whose annual tuition, accommodation and living costs vary from R25,000 to R40,000. The majority of students (80.5 per cent) indicated that the SRC should play a strong role in determining tuition fees.

The changing composition of students has changed that of the SRC. Compared to 1994 when only a handful of SRCs at HWUs and HWTs had black SRC members, all today have black SRC members, with the leadership of SRCs at most technikons today being composed solely of black students. One consequence is that black (African) students hold about 80 per cent of leadership positions at HE institutions. Along with the increase in the number of international students (who numbered 42,000 in 2002) some of these students (about 2 per cent) come from African countries other than South Africa. One other interesting demographic aspect relates to the small number of black women members at HBUs vs. the larger number of women at Afrikaans universities. For example, from 2000 to 2003 UDW had four women SRC members whereas the University of Potchefstroom had 20. This difference, *inter alia*, is partly a result of SASCO's failure to implement its ANC derived resolution (except in the Eastern Cape) that 30 per cent of its SRC members should be female. More broadly, research results show that student leaders attribute the low level of female participation at HBUs and HBTs to culture and lack of interest in student politics among female students.[11]

Student Participation: A Historical Overview

Historically, students were excluded from participating in decision-making at higher education institutions in South Africa although they nonetheless contested governance at institutions. From the outset, governance structures at universities were exclusionary in the sense that Council included business and state representatives but excluded student representatives. At historically black institutions (HBUs) where all-white councils were appointed by the State President (Kgware 1977).

Overall, this composition, at HBUs reflected the limited role then assigned to blacks at universities. Most HBUs were established in 1960. Initially, legislation provided for two main types of racially differentiated governance structures at these newly established institutions: a white council, a black advisory council, a white senate and a black advisory senate (Kgware 1977). These racially exclusive formations were opposed by staff at several institutions who called for mixed bodies that did not duplicate functions (Bhana 1977). Along with this external control over HBUs, in particular, the activities of SRCs were more tightly controlled. In the 1960s, SRC constitutions at some black universities were invariably written by management and required that SRCs restrict their roles to social, academic and administrative concerns (Maseko 1994). In doing this, SRC members represented students at functions, were viewed as ambassadors of institutions and occasionally selected by institutional managers. This often gave rise to resentment and meant that SRC members at black universities were sometimes viewed as stooges (Bhana 1977).

Where SRCs existed, the scope of their functions was limited since several institutions and government demanded that student actions be subject to their approval. At times, this contributed to the student view that the existence of SRCs implied student acceptance of government restrictions (see Bhana 1977, van der Ross 1977). In other cases, students refused to form SRCs on terms that did not suit them (Maseko 1994). This policy of non-collaboration presented councils with numerous challenges since various student bodies implicitly rejected the legal basis on which councils governed institutions. Apartheid higher education institutional governance structures (in particular councils) were accordingly often described as illegitimate and unrepresentative, and viewed as 'objects of resentment' (Badat 1999).

For students, this had enormous implications. White universities were effectively state-aided institutions[12] while black universities were ethnic institutions. Since each was further controlled externally (despite the existence of institutional autonomy) students' ability to influence institutional processes was always limited and to some extent dependent on national political changes. In response, student dissent and national student political movements have been a feature of the South African higher education landscape since the early 1920s. The National Union of South African Students (NUSAS), founded in 1924, presents the first example of a national student political movement that struggled over several decades to increase student influence at universities.[13] Mostly, this struggle was first carried by SRCs at English white and black universities[14] and by left-oriented clubs and societies that were influenced by Stalinist, Trotskyite and Leninist philosophies. Small liberal student groupings also often expressed a normative opposition to discriminatory practices or policies that limited individual actions.

This opposition took three principal forms:

1) SRCs generally accepted their role as voice institutions and represented student views on administrative and academic issues (in conjunction with student-based faculty boards and class representatives on academic issues to deans and senate).

2) SRCs and other student bodies addressed the implications of administrative decisions related to timetables, accommodation, tuition and residence fees with Registrars and other secretariat-level staff.

3) SRCs and other student bodies used protest action to highlight their opinions on policies regarding enrolment, discrimination, government policies and other social and political issues.

This last set of actions contributed to some SRCs rejecting the ideological-political basis upon which black universities, in particular, were established and to propositions that SRCs were weapons for the promotion of student activism and not merely structures that represented students on academic and administrative matters (Maseko 1994; Badat 1999). It is significant to note that the formation of the most significant black student political organization, the South African Students Organization (SASO) in 1968 resulted in calls for a black principal, black wardens, black representation on student disciplinary committees and on university planning committees, black representation on senates, and black representation on councils (Kgware 1977; van der Ross 1977). Students, at a small number of institutions, also took up the cudgels and engaged in violent confrontation with police and security officers to back up their claims. By the mid-1980s, this partly led to the branding of SRCs at some HBUs as creations of political formations and as subordinates to political student organizations and organs of 'people's power' (Gwala 1987; Maseko 1994).

A periodic effect, this consequence is a function of the rejection of the idea that SRCs in the 1970s and 1980 play the role of a liaison organ for institutions that communicate student grievances.[15]

Instead, SRCs at some HBUs came to be viewed as conscientization structures that informed students about the false ideology they previously internalised and facilitated their empowerment.[16] In this formulation, student leaders were strongly influenced by the views of Paulo Freire, Lenin and development theorists that highlighted participation as a key mechanism through which to effect empowerment. Accordingly, SRCs in the 1970-1994 period essentially functioned as cultural institutions that initiated student protest activities, provided the cultural-political unifiers (as legitimately elected representative structures) to lead students and influence university structures.

Collectively, these functions increased the social role of SRCs and the areas in which SRCs represented students. For example, these areas were no longer simply restricted to university concerns. The areas instead incorporated national concerns (Cele *et al* 2001). Further, they were political and economic in nature and intended to unify all students in common action, rather than highlight sectional or non-universal cultural concerns.[17] Thus, by the late 1980s, student demands had expanded into calls for the creation of the new and alternative 'organs of people power'.[18] This demand applied to all spheres of South African society, but in higher education institutions, it included calls for the establishment of broad transformation forums (BTFs) to democratise universities and to increase black influence. In addition, students argued that there was a need to democratise councils and senates by changing the composition and representation of constituencies and by allowing for decision-making processes that were democratic and participatory (NCHE 1996).

Following concerted protest and institutional struggles to establish black-led SRCs and to participate in institutional decision-making, these last demands were eventually conceded in the early 1990s. The initial vehicles were Broad Transformation Forums (BTF's).[19] These structures which brought together worker, student, civil society, academic and management representatives emerged at almost all institutions to help restore confidence in governance, to contain conflict and to legitimate efforts aimed at institutional transformation.[20] Among the few universities at which BTFs were not established, the University of Stellenbosch (US) stands out as an institution which had very close ties to the ruling government and which subsequently changed institutional management structures, policies, programmes and staff composition at a snails pace. Beyond this, few BTFs were formed at technikons due to the tight control management exerts at these institutions and the limited historic role that SRCs and non-business representatives played.

They sprung from the continued efforts by students at specifically black universities to discredit management, to contest fee increases, to demand increased access to institutions, better accommodation, different governance structures and the involvement of 'people's representatives' in institutional activities[21] (Johnson 2000).

Collectively, this challenged management's prerogative to make decisions without adequate consultation and without the involvement of those most affected by decisions. Mostly the organized groups such as students, workers and unionized academics argued that effective participation is one of the key criteria of any democratic process and that democracy and increased involvement of black staff were crucial in effectively steering higher education institutions. In this sense, the introduction of a higher education cooperative governance model was intended to forge a new political process or culture of democracy within the system.

The philosophical underpinnings of this model were wide-ranging and not reducible to a single set of views, but everyone upheld Dahl's (1989: 109) postulate that throughout the process of making binding decisions, citizens ought to have an adequate and equal opportunity for expressing their preferences as to the final outcome. For Dahl, this meant that, the students must have adequate and equal opportunities for placing questions on the agenda and for expressing reasons for endorsing one outcome rather than another. To deny any citizen adequate opportunities for effective participation means that because their preferences are unknown or incorrectly perceived, they cannot be taken into account.

For students this meant that SRCs should be the vehicles through which their views about fee increases, accommodation, academic programmes and the like were presented. This, they argued, should not occur after fee increases or other actions affecting students, but before. They added that consultation and advice-seeking actions should be a necessary cornerstone of institutional governance (Johnson 2000). Badat (1999: 25) and Wolpe (1989: 23) argue that the formation of structures and relations is always the outcome of struggles between contending groups or classes. For Badat (1999), this implies that the analysis of the outcomes, success and failure of organizational initiatives and collective action as well as understanding the form and content of struggles should be grounded on the conditions underpinning the struggles. For students, this further meant that BTFs had to address institutional culture and they themselves should be involved in shaping the vision and mission of institutions and contributing to planning frameworks.

In this regard, students clearly linked the demand for institutional change and the establishment of BTFs to broader restructuring processes occurring within South African society. In several fundamental respects, the demand for BTFs duplicated other reform processes. At national government level, parallel processes from 1992 to 1994 resulted in the formation of Interim councils that examined broad transformation issues and tried to steer the direction of change. These negotiations were underpinned by the view that stakeholders should jointly engage around issues, try to resolve points of difference and lay down processes through which structured change could be effected. At national government level, this provided a framework for co-operative governance and joint decision-making by business, labour, government and the government-in-waiting.

More narrowly, the culture of cooperative governance is part of the broader reconstruction of the higher education process against the backdrop of rampant globalization. This has contributed to institutions developing new missions and visions and has accelerated both corporatism and stronger management-type steering of higher education institutions. The new government elected in 1994 further took up this broad theme of representative democracy and central steering by requiring that institutions make provision for accommodating student leaders in institutional structures. Indeed, with the election of a new government, student participation is increasingly seen as central to the development and sustainability of an acceptable and effective institutional governance structures and decision-making processes. This last point was recognized during the NCHE process when the role of BTFs was more narrowly defined to embrace institutional issues only. This commission noted that new governance structures in higher education were necessary and that such structures should take the form of advisory bodies for restructuring and innovation where representatives of all stakeholders could meet, identify problems, mediate interests and advise relevant structures (NCHE 1996).

This view was later promoted by the government's comprehensive framework on transformation - the 1997 Education White Paper 3 and 1997 Higher Education Act 101 (DoE 1997). The 1997 White Paper dealt with South African responses to the challenges of institutional transformation within a global age. To deepen democracy and strengthen institutional management, the White Paper highlights the value of co-operative governance and encourages the 'meaningful involvement of students and staff in all permanent governance structures of the institutions including councils' (DoE 1997).

Principally, the 1997 Higher Education Act 101 overturned four decades of excluding black students at historically black universities from participating in institutional decision-making. The Act requires that all HE institutions formally recognize Student Representative Councils (SRCs) and approve their constitutions. The Act also provides elected student leaders with seats in the highest decision-making body on strategic issues (council), the highest academic body (senate) and the highest advisory body (Institutional Forums).

Regarding the manner of their involvement, the Act stipulates that students should act in the interest of the institution when participating in governance structures, and not act as mandate-carrying representatives from student organisations (see Ncayiyana and Hayward 1999: 46). This formulation aims to promote deliberative democracy (rational discussion and agreement). However, if voting is necessary to create agreement, students have to form alliances with other stakeholders and acquire further votes from HE managers to secure their preference. Fundamentally, the Act then did not dilute the power of institutional leaders. Rather, it promoted 'constructive engagement' between HE management and student leaders by facilitating the incorporation of student leaders.

Three primary factors underpinned this democratization process. First, the trickle down effect of the corporatist arrangements that characterized South Africa's post-1994 political transition created a framework for promoting co-operation between former political opponents. Second, the ANC government had sufficient political muscle and legitimacy amongst student leaders and the new group of HE managers – whose appointment the Minister of Education approved — to legislate their co-operation. As in other African countries (Munene 2003), the implication is that some students form part of the national political order. Third, government and HE managers viewed incorporation of students into governance structures as the most appropriate measure to 'professionalize' their actions and minimize annual bouts of protest and conflict, while simultaneously promoting democratic practice.

The consequences of this situation include student involvement in committees dealing with academic development, student fees, bursary allocations, institutional finances, financial exclusions, academic exclusions, appointing senior executives, equity committees and a host of other institutional structures. As in trade union contexts, the price SRCs were asked to pay for formal access to decision-making involved the possibility of being influenced by management and acting like an instrument of social order. The price therefore included the possibility of defending the decisions of HE managers vis-à-vis students and turning their back on the tried and tested means of dissent and mass protest because the ANC government and HE institutions desired stable academic processes.

Participation Experiences of Students

Since the change in national government in 1994, popular perception holds that student political activism at universities and technikons has declined. This is widely viewed as having contributed to stable institutional governance, fewer disruptions to academic programmes and to a decline in the incidence of protest actions. It is indeed so that the upsurge of publicly visible student political activism in the 1980s and early 1990s has given way to sporadic one-off protests on matters such as fee increases, exclusions, institutional racism, management's powers, mergers, and greater student participation in decision-making. In the same vein, students now play a more modest role limited to campaigning for a greater role in campus governance structures and exert no real influence on political events, but they are still interested in matters of social concern such as the rising incidence of HIV-Aids and increase in mortality.

Protest actions have nonetheless remained common at historically black institutions. In 1999 and 2000, students at the University of Durban Westville (UDW) protested against the exclusion of fellow students for financial reasons, while students at the University of the North burned barricades and alleged misappropriation of funds by members of the Students Representative Council (SRC). For the past three years, students at the University of Venda have protested against corruption and misspending by SRC members. In 2001, Fort Hare students protested following accusations that SRC leaders benefited from nepotistic institutional practices. In 2002, students at Natal University, University of Durban Westville, ML Sultan Technikon, Eastern Cape Technikon and University of Transkei protested against mergers, while students at the University of the North went on a rampage following suggestions that management would not concede to demands for the allocation of additional money for a bash. The Medical University of South Africa further closed for one week in February 2002 and one week in March, while the University of the North closed for one week in May. In 2003 lengthy interruptions to academic programmes also occurred at Fort Hare University where close to 1 000 students were excluded by the university authorities for failing to pay fees.

Protests in 2001 also manifested at historically white institutions where black students demanded changes to regulations for SRC candidates at the University of Potchefstroom and to the composition of the SRC at the University of Pretoria (UP). At the same time, white students protested last year against the use of English during a public meeting at Pretoria. Localism also characterized one-off incidents at the University of Stellenbosch (US) where a call for less public initiation rituals produced a one-off protest and at Technikon Natal where students protested that a merger with ML Sultan could devalue the quality of their qualification. On the other hand, broader social concerns played a key role at Wits where HIV/Aids awareness activities provided reasons for an anti-government protest, while for a few hundred students from the University of Cape Town (UCT), fees and restricted bursary opportunities provided an opportunity to express their frustration in 2001. In addition, in 2003, students at Witwatersrand Technikon protested against policies that limit sexual contact in residences, while race-based incidents occurred at the University of Stellenbosch and University of Pretoria. But not all protests have had a local dimension. Cross-national and international issues have also featured in public protest. In 2001 and in 2002, some students at the Cape Technikon, University of Stellenbosch, University of Cape Town, Rhodes University and Witwatersrand University marched in support of anti-farm evictions and pro-democracy activities in Zimbabwe while the Israeli-Palestine conflict continues to generate support for both sides with students on each side participating in placard demonstrations and marches at Wits.

However, while protest have remained a constant feature since 1994, student organizations have also changed the way they take up issues, their methods of mobilization and the way they respond to management. These adaptations have involved responding to external and internal developments, *inter alia*. For example, portfolios on SRCs have changed. Following the promulgation of mergers, several SRCs have created portfolios for Merger Officers[22] by shuffling responsibilities between different portfolios. Another example relates to the disappearance of the Political and Education portfolios that existed during the 1980s and early 1990s. These positions were invariably replaced with Transformation and Equity Officers, while many SRCs also added Culture and Entertainment portfolios to the services they provide to students to cater for the demand for more social activities. To effectively participate in governance structures, SRCs have also had to select individuals to represent them on particular structures and have had to provide space for this.

Besides this type of positional change, other adaptations have involved developing policy-making structures to ensure that student politics could participate in institutional affairs irrespective of whether or not an SRC existed. At some institutions such developments involved the establishment of a Student Parliament consisting of representatives from cultural, sports, academic and political student organizations that are required to discuss strategic approaches to problems faced by students. But not all have chosen to create fixed structures for this purpose. Thus, the University of the Western Cape relies on a Student Summit – a one-off annual event at which recognized role players participate and help chart responses to issues facing students. The overall effect of these structures has been to shift the focus of communication in SRCs from engagement in a mass meeting (potentially with all students) to organizational engagement and greater organizational involvement in institutional governance structures with the SRC, in most cases, playing the role of coordinator of student decision-making.

Furthermore, organizational developments have involved changes in the relationship between SRC members and ordinary students. This engagement was often direct, with SRC members 'manning' offices and making themselves available to assist students. While this element still exists, some SRCs have created 'service providers' (sub-committees comprising of students) that address particular needs and respond to queries. Where this exists, the SRC itself mainly functions as an administrative body that deals with correspondence and liaison issues, while the service provider interacts with 'ordinary' students and provides a 'professional' service in a designated domain. Where this has occurred, SRC members have subsequently indicated that they have 'lost contact' with students, but believe that the development is a logical consequence of three factors: first, a lack of interest in student political matters; second the under-resourcing of SRCs in terms of funding sufficient administrative positions; the increasing need for SRC members to attend institutional committee meetings in order to remain informed of institutional developments and to communicate this to students.

During interviews student leaders further indicated that participation in governance structures has largely involved a focus on adhering to procedures and did not really addressed outcome issues. At all the institutions, the main emphasis has been on adapting to the changing organizational context and trying to learn what student organizations should do. For student leaders, this adaptation has generally involved paying much greater attention to management issues since their roles, at one extreme, appear to involve considerable office functions. Indicative of this, student leaders we interviewed indicated that the SRCs they participate in have more formal bureaucratic features than before, that they are generally understaffed and involve an increasing number of official activities. For them this means that they perform a wide range of administrative duties and act as 'professional counselors to those who voted for them' and as 'management consultants' to the university executive who they keep informed of student decisions and possible actions. The reasons for these two perspectives and their implications are in many ways self-evident. Since student leaders interact with university and technikon management they are knowledgeable about institutional policies and in a position to inform other students. Second, they are trusted – because they were elected – and are believed to act in the interests of students, whereas other university officials are widely viewed as putting bureaucratic interests first. Third, their involvement in institutional meetings involves carrying student views and putting student perspectives on issues.

But, while process issues have featured strongly in student participation, they have not always participated equally. One reason relates to poor attendance. This is attributed in some institutions to 'leaders not showing enough responsibility' and in other institutions to student leaders being "overworked" since they mostly remain full-time students, but sometimes serve on more than 10 institutional committees, while also being involved in SRC activity and in the work of their student organization. But, poor attendance in meetings also relates to the fact that student leaders sit on consultative structures that lack decision-making powers. For example, one common student's comment highlights the point that Institutional Forums were 'toothless' and only active when faced with senior appointments and re-naming buildings and structures. A second gripe involves students' difficulty in dealing with issues, documents, deliberations in senates that do not deal with "fancy issues" such as governance, but with hard academic issues, which in most instances would have gone through long.[23]

In these cases, student leaders highlighted a central criticism that SRCs are often expected by management representatives to advance only mandated positions from the student body or at least to speak more on issues which directly concern the general student body and not to contribute to general issues. A further perceived expectation relates to a perception that student participation in governance structures is exploited to legitimate decisions since their limited voting power does not provide for veto rights, while they often have no real chance of influencing decisions. For this reason, student leaders evaluated their participation as not being robust and as characterized by their silence on issues in which they are expected to speak on. In general, they speak mostly on issues which have a direct impact on students such as fees, access, the appointment of senior management especially the vice-chancellor, etc. But there was also a feeling that students reserve their comments on things that they are comfortable with.

What have students achieved through participation? This question elicited varied responses. Mainly staff and students suggested that students have displayed mature leadership and shown that protest was not the sole means through which change could be effected. For them, this change in tactics produced the following results across the five institutions: Student leadership has worked with management in establishing common frameworks around which future negotiations around student access, retention, exclusion and individual financial difficulties could be addressed. This involved extended negotiations for several years in forums outside council, senate and IFs, but was greatly helped by participation in such forums since students participated in relaying the outcome of negotiations. The 'pacts' in turn provide a platform for future engagement around issues and implies that 'institutional memory' and not 'strength' will determine the outcome of future engagements around access, retention and exclusion.

Student leaders have continually provided a student perspective on issues and highlighted historical trajectories with respect to how some issues affect students and how they have historically been handled differently. This, in the view of students, has contributed to several important victories. For example, all institutions have lately raised tuition and residence fees substantially, but student leaders feel that they have been able to contest the scale of tuition fee increases and are responsible, in cases, for lower than envisaged increases.

Involvement with management representatives has contributed to student leaders establishing up joint bursary and tuition support schemes to support needy students. This has increased the scope of SRC activities and has contributed to SRC members playing a greater role as part of the corporate face of institutions. It has also meant that their overall contribution to institutional investments has greatly expanded.

Student leaders have gained from the presentation of 'institutional pictures' in forums and have gained a greater appreciation of long-standing institutional efforts to promote student welfare. They have specifically gained greater insight into budgetary concerns and issues that impact on institutional performance and have been able to look at the way developments impact on the institution, and not simply on students. This in turn has meant that they have tried to defend student interests in a more guarded manner and have not necessarily contested issues that the larger student body views as crucial.

Student leaders have represented foreign students and other student views and experiences in consultation with management representatives and have consistently been able to push a student position and to improve the position of sectional student groups. This has especially happened at UCT and Stellenbosch.

Student leaders have developed and improved administrative and policy skills. They have gained familiarity with national priority issues confronting institutions such as the scope and content of debates, the development of three-year strategic plans. They have also helped shape the vision embodied in institutional responses to nation-wide developments.

However, others expressed discontent and disillusionment with their participation in policy and institutional governance issues. They described their participation as debilitating since their views are often not taken very seriously. This is most forcibly expressed in the following argument:

> Student participation is a joke. There is a mentality that students are about protests. We are capable of causing violence and bringing institutions into turmoil. We are not seen as intellectually capable to contribute to transformation, but are expected to listen to senior professors. ... Most of the time we attend to get information about what is happening. No agenda is given. No preparation takes place. No mandate is carried. ... Although we don't fully participate, it is really better to get access to information, than to abstain and remaining ignorant. Sometimes we don't understand the issues under discussion. ... With finance issues we wait for stuff around students and then contribute. Otherwise our views don't matter. Some see us as delaying decision-making.[24]

On the other hand, there are comments indicating that student leaders are expected to participate equally in committee meetings and to be actively involved in deliberations, but are hamstrung by the onerous demands of full participation.

Asked what organizational difficulties student leaders and structures encounter in responding to the changing political landscape, several interviewees noted that while unevenness exists across institutions, leadership, policy training and research expertise were essential and that official skills require improvement. Their tasks are further complicated by the fact that in some cases, previous SRCs did not keep adequate records, that they lack information about the terms of agreements reached with university management; and that there was little continuity in the handing over of positions.[25] Consequently, SRCs members are not always fully prepared for the responsibilities they have to assume and the tasks they have to perform. Many also lack experience in staffing organizations and do not have a clear idea of what they need to do in their various portfolios, or what possible strategies they could follow to improve organizational performance. As a result members conceded that they often flounder in meetings with university management, feel powerless in representing students and need training in organizational procedures and university protocols.[26]

In their defense, several students also noted that bureaucratic difficulties were similar to problems experienced by earlier SRCs, but that new benchmarks existed in terms of financial accountability and proper reports and that there were many formal demands. For them, the enormity of this adaptation requires socialization into new organizational practices. Thus, whereas lax accounting procedures were sometimes tolerated in the past, to circumvent misspending, audited statements brought tighter controls and formal accountability in performing tasks. Others noted that besides administrative difficulties, it is arduous to mobilize students in support of actions and unlikely that protest action could be sustained for a few days without incidents of violence. While it happened in 2003 that protest action at the University of Fort Hare and Witwatersrand Technikon lasted for extended periods, this partly related to institutions being closed to take the sting out of protest and to limit the damage caused by newspaper reports of disruptions. Flowing from this, interviewees intimated that SRCs were responding to pressure from small groups when mobilizing students and that proper representation of concerns through appropriate channels is time-consuming, frustrating and exhausting.

Further compounding administration and governance difficulties is the fact that portfolios were not always neatly aligned with emerging responsibilities, but that constitutional changes were difficult to make as apathy made it difficult to get quorums.[27] Also, SRC members conceded that they needed to do a situation analysis to determine how best to address student issues. Instead they inherited organizational frameworks and operated within their parameters. Consequently, when new issues arose, responses were haphazard or characterized by inaction, as it was not always clear who was responsible for taking up specific issues or how this should be done. Also while SRCs are now more involved in policy considerations than before, they lack knowledge of legislative frameworks and policy processes. Nor do their budgets allow for commissioned research or other assistance when engaging in policy actions, yet, they and other student representatives are expected to participate in committees dealing with appointments, employment equity and transformation issues. In consequence, several SRCs have requested that leadership skills, project management, entrepreneurial management, skills training and capacity building programmes should be institutionalized and that they receive training in administrative management and policy related issues.

Student leaders or organizations have recently deployed ethnicity and racism as a student election strategy. During the 2002/2003 UWC SRC elections, the issue of ethnicity featured prominently as a tool to highlight the plight of coloured students and the need to unify students under the broader umbrella of the United Student Front, on the one hand. On the other hand, it was used as a 'conscious strategy' to unseat SASCO, which seemed to have a numerical advantage over individual opposition groups. In this regard, SASCO was projected especially through its nominated list of candidates as an organization that did not accommodate other ethnic groups than Xhosa group. Illustrating this, an argument was raised both during interviews we conducted and anonymous pamphlet issued during elections that the current and only SASCO member in the SRC was supposed to be nominated as a presidential candidate. But he was not nominated because he was not a Xhosa. There were issues about the way SASCO SRC operated and use of SRC vehicles, offices, etc. The interviews further indicated that ethnicity is not a mere political ploy.

> What happened, I think was a card that was used by our opposition. There was a time whereby there was a flyer that was circulated on campus pretending to be from a member of SASCO whereby the article said that I as this member of SASCO is concerned by the way the organization is Nguni dominated, it is Xhosa. There is ethnicity within SASCO. If you are not Xhosa you are going to be marginalized in SASCO. So that was the perception that created around campus by the opposition camouflaged to be a member of SASCO writing that article. Then there was a debate around the issue of ethnicity with people saying that SASCO is an ethnic group. That people from the Eastern Cape, Xhosas, dominate the SRC in particular. But also when you go back to the history, previous leadership, it is not true. SASCO never condoned or encouraged issues of ethnic divisions because we are a non-racial, non-sexist organization. So we accommodate each and everyone. But one issue we have never done is to say we are going to give specific treatment to particular groupings. We deploy

> comrades equally. We are not going to deploy you because you are coloured. We deploy you on the basis that you are committed enough to take a job. Because it is a public office. What you do in the office is always going to reflect back on SASCO. They are not going to say it is XXXX who is doing bad, they are going to say its SASCO.[28]

In addition, ethnicity and racism have manifested themselves in various ways — be it among students, between students and staff or between students and senior managers. One UWC SRC member argued that some students (particularly Coloured) were not welcome and and did not have a sense of belonging to the campus. It was argued that these students had 'limited access to resources' such as financial aid and so forth.

> It's a perception of I'm not black enough. I categorized as black but I'm not black. It's an issue if I need funding or financial assistance. The university will not give it to me because I am financially…and the issue of the work-study needs to be looked at, and be addressed. It's the fact that coloured students feel they are here merely…space and not here create a constructive contribution like the fact that Indian students sit at the library and congregate. I have money, I don't need to associate myself with coloured students, and I don't have to associate with Black students, because their problems are not my problems. It is an issue that students should stop to syndicate themselves into little quarantines, and say my issues are special, my issues are special, my issues are not student issues.[29]

While another SRC member argued that some African students perceive Coloured students as being given preferential treatment with regard to bursary allocation and interactions with academics at UWC. To this extent, there are:

> More African students than coloured students who go through the university credit management control in order to be cleared before proceeding to register. In addition students from other African countries seem not to be treated the same way as those from the rest of the world. For example, a group of African students had to wait for three to four days before they could be allocated individual rooms. Whereas non-African students did not experience the same problem, everything was sorted out before they could even arrive on campus.[30]

Regarding the issue of ethnicity at UCT, a SRC member[31] indicated that some students (particularly African) view residence admission and allocation policies as being ethnic-based. In terms of these policies, a priority is given to those students (mainly white) with the best matric results, mainly from ex-model C schools.

At UDW, the issue of ethnicity has been used as a political mobilisation strategy by the 2002/2003 SRC president to mobilize students to oppose his suspension from the university. That was after charges of corruption, bribery, fraud and coercing the institution to enter into contracts costing the university millions of rands and mismanagement of university funds were leveled against the president by the university management. Subsequently, a series of student placard demonstrations were held, calling for the immediate reinstatement of the SRC president. In addition, it was alleged that the SRC president was 'responsible for a pamphlet, which was distributed on campus accusing Cooper of creating an "Indostan" by appointing management that is predominantly Indian".[32] The SRC president argued that 'while we agree with the content of the pamphlet, the SRC would not have raised those issues by distributing anonymous pamphlets'.[33]

He questioned the appointment of the new vice-chancellor, describing the move as a blow to the transformation goals of higher education institutions. He said that he was being 'victimized because I questioned the appointment of the vice-chancellor'.[34]

Although about 57 per cent of the students disagreed that the SRC is mainly for hostel or residence students. In most institutions, students who reside outside campuses (and part-time and distance) seem to be neglected and not integrated into SRC activities in effective and meaningful ways. To this extent, at UDW township students organized themselves and formed a township student society to handle with transport, representation and other issues. At the University of the North, postgraduate students established their association as an alternative form of student representation. A similar initiative was aborted at UCT mainly because the SRC opposed it. According to the UCT SRC, had this attempt succeeded it would have seriously threatened and challenged the relevance and role of SRC structures. Given failure in launching postgraduate associations, postgraduate students have in most institutions resorted to contest the SRC elections and to use them as a forum for voicing their grievances; whether this is effective remains to be investigated.

The lack of sufficient involvement of all students is mainly due to the fact that most SRC constitutions are not respected and applied with respect to the composition of the SRC. The UDW SRC should consist of 26 members (house committees, faculty councils, part-time students, clubs and societies and executive members, with nine members directly elected annually by the general student body). However, this has never happened; instead the SRC is usually composed of the nine executive. At UCT SRC is an executive arm of the Student Parliament, which was described as being ineffective and needing to be changed. There seems to be tension between the role and powers of the SRC and Student Parliament. The tension is caused by the fact that SRC members are elected directly by the general student body, whereas membership to Student Parliament is through indirect nomination or recommendation from various clubs and societies representing sectoral interests. The SRC has found it difficult to accept the fact that it was accountable to the student parliament despite the fact that it was directly elected by the student body.

Gererally, SRCs strive to attract as many students as possible to participate in their activities. This was evident in the response of 55.6 per cent of students who felt that there was far too little involvement in SRC affairs. SRCs have been organizing bashes with a view to drawing support and meeting social needs of students. Students' interest in attending bashes is flagging to the extent that both the UWC and UCT recently organized a joint bash held at the UWC sports stadium. But this event failed to attract thousands of students from both campuses in spite of the fact that about 87.5 per cent of students felt that the SRC should become more active in promoting social and reaction activities for students. The failure of this joint social activity was due to the prohibitive entrance fees (R30) that most students could not afford to pay[35] and perhaps because students need more religious or cultural festivals and so forth.[36] It was also argued that SRCs entertainment activities usually cater for resident students at the expense of the broader student body. Thus, students in hostels are unfortunately African students and as a result coloured students do not participate. Therefore one of the key immediate challenges is to attract coloured students to participate in entertainment activities, but 'I had no idea how to do that'.[37]

Students felt that the SRC should play a more active role in the following areas: About 61.2 per cent strongly felt that the SRC should play an important role in promoting democracy on campuses. About 83.2 per cent strongly felt that the SRC should protect and advance their interests. About 84.8 per cent strongly felt that the SRC should represent their interests. About 66.2 per cent strongly felt that the SRC should be accountable to students. About 63.4 per cent strongly felt that the SRC should promote debates on racialism on campus. About 28.3 per cent strongly felt that the SRC should promote political debates on campus. About 52.8 per cent strongly felt that the SRC should promote debates on the economy. About 41.5 per cent strongly felt that the SRC should not be linked to any political organization. About 20.8 per cent strongly felt that part-time and distance students should elect their own SRC representatives. About 58.3 per cent strongly felt that the SRC members should be available on a full time basis to address student issues. About 42.8 per cent felt that SRC members are providing competent leadership on campus. About 52.2 per cent were not sure if the SRC was autocratic on campus. About 56.3 per cent felt that the lack of involvement in important student issues was a real problem on their campus. About 49 per cent felt that SRC should play strong role in political activities on campus. About 88.1 per cent felt the SRC should play a strong role in academic activities on. About 90.4 per cent felt that the SRC should play a strong role in addressing safety and security for students on campus. About 81.5 per cent felt that the SRC should play a strong role in addressing HIV/AIDS-related issues on campus. About 72.8 per cent felt that the SRC should establish good relations with other structures on campus. About 74.3 per cent felt that the SRC should become more active in taking up women's issues. About 69.2 per cent felt that the SRC should become more active in addressing transport and parking issues. About 85.7 per cent felt that the SRC should become more active in addressing disability issues.

Conclusion and Recommendations

What the preceding description highlights is that student organizations have adapted to the changing higher education environment over the last ten years and that they have acted as 'learning organizations'. However, while they have adapted to changes in governance structures and to different aspirations from their constituency, a key question remains: what have they achieved and why?

The implications of this question are important. If student organizations have not achieved much through their participation, an important issue is whether they can achieve more by adopting a different approach. Indeed, there is a widely held view that student organizations are more likely to score 'victories' on challenges confronting students if they engaged in protest action, despite the vehemence with which many university and technikon interest groups reject protest action nowadays. In this perspective, protest action immediately draws institutional attention to an issue and requires that the issue be resolved. Since students invariably occupy the moral high ground because their inability to pay fees or academic performance partly relates to a failure from government to adequately provide for their needs, it is opined that they are invariably likely to win protests around financial, academic and transformation concerns.

In addressing this issue, student leaders variously indicated that the changing nature of the student body and the diverse aspirations of students mean that they cannot simply act in the interests of particular constituencies, and that this has affected the manner in which resource struggles are addressed. They further suggested that the fundamental problem they encounter is that HE institutions have not fully transformed themselves and that institutions also cannot realistically solve societal problems such as the ability of working class learners to pay their fees. In their view, HE institutions have, for the most part, done their best to respond to student demands, although they have not necessarily responded speedily and without being pressurized to act in a particular manner. What further stands out in their responses is that the responses have largely been in line with government policies, some of which have been contested in student ranks. This has led to strong interest in demographic change and in how financially sound institutions are managed because this is in the national interest. In this regard, emphasis has been placed on programmatic, and therefore, gradual change in dealing with issues such as responsiveness to labour market demands, devising strategies to ensure that student debt is reduced and HE institutions become more financially autonomous.

What this in turn has done is raise an interesting dilemma: with some exceptions, the effect of student actions over the last few years, and of their participation in governance structures, has contributed to more stable governance patterns and adaptation to pre-emptive approaches to potential conflict resolution without resort to protest (and violence). This has been in line with the view that student organizations should act as a complement to the policies of the government and in support of national political efforts to steer the higher education system more closely in order to ensure that future labour-market needs are met. But, along with this, HE institutions have also increasingly raised their fees, become selective in who they admit and have generally moved in the direction of treating students as customers who pay for specific services. In this sense, the privatization and individualization of HE services has actually run parallel to efforts to realize national interests, which raises the question whether the larger student bodies are best served by student political organizations or by independent candidates whose interest lies in winning popularity contests and in promoting socially-oriented interests.

Recommendations or Policy Options

Establishment of National Student Federation
Students need to strengthen their influence and contribution to national debates and policy process. Critical to this is the establishment of united and legitimate body representing and carrying the mandates of all students, irrespective of political affiliation, race, gender, institutional affiliation, etc.

More Broadly Representative and Expanded Student Representative Councils (SRCS)
There is no doubt that the current student governance system is inadequate and incapable of realizing such broad objectives of democracy, accountability, active participation, transparency and delivery of student needs. Therefore, rather than disband or cast SRCs as irrelevant and irresponsible structures, government should establish an expanded and broadly representative system of student governance that allows more students to participate and actually influence SRC decisions and orientations.

Systematic and Coherent Capacity-Building Programme
One of the key challenges facing students which they themselves acknowledged is the lack of necessary and appropriate capacity to lead, drive and shape policy at both national and institutional level, and to robustly engage in all debates, includ-

ing academic programmes and curriculum. Both national government and higher education institutions need to be responsible for developing students' capacity. Accordingly advanced and systematic capacity-building programmes should be established and implemented.

Political Education Revival Programme
The three national student political organizations (South African Congress, Azanian Student Congress and Pan Africanist Student Movement) are facing serious political challenges internally and externally. These organizations are facing serious problems such as dwindling of resources, lack of quality and visionary leadership, and membership. Furthermore, their credibility and legitimacy are challenged on the grounds of their performance as SRCs on campuses. Some of the external challenges are linked to the nature of the current crop of students characterized as being politically unconscious, young, consumerist and individualistic. There is also a large group of students from the emerging black bourgeoisie and middle class who attended better and well resourced schools and, unlike the majority of their black fellow students, are not faced with the huge financial problems which have triggered most student protests and boycotts.

Student political organizations therefore need a serious comprehensive education and revival programme to enhance their role and relevance.

Student Unity and Social Cohesion Programme
The creation and realization of a non-racial, democratic and non-sexist society means that higher education should produce students imbued with these values. Issues of race, gender, ethnic differences and discrimination are still predominant in our society and manifest themselves in various ways, including student power and leadership struggles. There is need therefore for higher education authorities and all key stakeholders, including students, to create and promote student unity and social cohesion across the spectrum.

Notes
1. This article was written in 2004
2. See detailed discussion on this in the 1997 ANC Strategy and Tactics document.
3. See details government Ten Year Review 2003 (Endnotes)
4. South African Student Congress Annual Congress Political Report (1996:12)
5. Charles van Onselen (1997)
6. (Nkomo 1984, Badat 1999)
7. Cele, G., Koen, C., Mabizela, M. (2001) 'Student Politics and Higher Education in South Africa - Emerging Trends since the early 1990s'. Paper presented at the EPU/ SRHE conference on Globalisation and Higher Education. March. Cape Town.
8. Cape Talk. "Latham at Six", Thursday, 9 March 2001- Gerda Kruger. Similar descriptions have characterised the responses of university spokespersons at other institutions. For example, UDW ascribed activities leading to the fatal shooting of a student last year as

the work of troublemakers who managed to disrupt university activities.
9. Cooper and Subotzky, 2001.
10. Bunting, I. (2003) "Foreign Students and Academic Staff in Public Higher Education in South Africa in 2001", In Pillay, P. et al., (Eds) "GATS and Higher Education in SADC.
11. (see NASDEV's 2002: Women in Leadership survey).
12. All institutions have historically depended on government for financing. Thus, while institutional autonomy is centrally inscribed in South African higher education, the state has always been able to influence institutional policies and to prescribe the framework within which institutions operate.
13. NUSAS was widely perceived to be a national student political body, but was actually constituted as a federation of SRCs at white English universities. In this sense, only SRC members were actually members of NUSAS. More broadly, NUSAS developed a broad political manifesto and covertly organized student activities through SRCs or other structures at white English universities.
14. SRC members were largely drawn from the ranks of national student political organisations. At English universities this contributed to NUSAS dominating student politics. At Afrikaans universities, individuals associated with the Afrikaanse Studente Bond (formed in 1934 at three institutions) did the same. In later periods, students from organizations such as the South African Student Organization (SASO) and Azanian Student Organization (AZASO) and South African National Student Congress (SANSCO) did much the same. Breakaway groups from these organizations and groups that either positioned itself to the left or right sometimes dominated the SRC for short periods at some institutions, but also fulfilled a similar role.
15. A similar response emerged in trade union circles where efforts were increasingly made to organize black workers into industrial unions whose power derived from shop stewards. This lead to the replacement of management appointed liaison councils with more effective worker representatives who tackled industrial and societal issues. In this regard, it is clear that obvious parallels exist between student struggles and broader economic struggles and that these conflicts did not occur in isolation of each other.
16. This role was linked to divisions in student bodies and the fact that not all students agreed that SRCs should play a wider political role. Indeed, while not covered in literature, apathy contributed to the failure of many SRC elections at several universities during the 1970s. It also contributed to some SRCs devoting energy to ensure the success of future elections. This involved building organizational structures, rather than focusing most energy on conscientization activities. At some institutions, activism was also seen in a negative light since it contributed to high failure rates, brought interruptions to the academic programme and contributed to increased violent outbursts at institutions.
17. Students at HBUs unanimously demanded the replacement of the existing government with democratically elected representatives who committed themselves to promoting the aims of a non-racial democracy. At some institutions, this political demand was linked to economic restructuring. Opinions were divided on the form this should take. Students at some institutions strongly supported a socialist economy while others favoured more market-driven policies.
18. This conceptualisation showed strong support for the African National Congress (ANC) and the South African Communist Party (SACP) in student ranks. Principally, the ANC

advocated the use of people's power to drive a wedge between those who supported and those who opposed the struggle for a non-racial democracy. The people's power notion further held that individuals and collectives could influence social change by standing together in pursuit of social justice.
19. These structures were, at the time, widely viewed as having a status comparable to that of senate and council. However, whereas senates and councils were viewed as tainted by their historic roles, BTFs were perceived by students (and worker representatives) as legitimate structures that would drive change at higher education institutions.
20. Among the few universities at which BTFs were not established, the University of Stellenbosch (US) stands out as an institution which had very close ties to the ruling government and which subsequently changed institutional management structures, policies, programmes and staff composition at a snails pace. Beyond this, few BTFs were formed at technikons due to the tight control management exerts at these institutions and the limited historic role that SRCs and non-business representatives played.
21. The fact that some SRCs and student bodies strongly articulated these demands resulted in them effectively setting the agenda of many BTFs meetings (see Johnson, 2000 for a description of the key role students played at UWC). At other institutions, the BTFs were steered much more centrally by institutional managers and were used to achieve the same decision-legitimating outcome (see Austin, 2001 in King and Mabokela, 2001 for a description of the role management played at UPE).
22. The term 'merger' refers to the government amalgamation and reduction of higher education institutions from 36 to 23.
23. See Hardy, C., Langley, A., Mintzberg, H. and Rose, J. (2001) "Strategy Formation in the University Setting" In Jenniskens, I., eds., "Management and Decision-Making in Higher Education Institutions", CHEPS and CHERI, pp.293-325.
24. Cele et al., Ref 4
25. Here UCT SRC represented the sole exception. Most notably minutes of last years meetings are logged on an internet site and are available along with other historical information and information from newsletters.
26. Interviewees at all institutions expressed this sense of powerlessness. In addition, interviewees at four institutions indicated uncertainty about tasks. SRC members at three institutions revealed that they were particularly unsure about demands since they had no idea what was expected of them in some forums (that have existed for several years).
27. These factors have especially been cited at WITS and at UWC with the latter being forced to operate with a draft constitution adopted in 1997.
28. Interview held on March 27, 2003
29. Interview with UWC SRC member, March 20, 2003
30. Interview with UWC SRC member, March 20, 2003).
31. Interview held on March 31, 2003
32. 2003 March 19 The Mercury
33. Mercury Ref.19
34. Mercury Ref. 19
35. UWC SRC member, March 21, 2003
36. UWC SRC member 2003 March 20c, UCT SRC member, March 31, 2003.

37. Interview: Ref.16

Bibliography

Badat, S., 1999, *Black Student Politics – from SASO to SANSCO, 1968-1990*, Pretoria: Human Science Research Council.

Badat, S., Barends, Z. and Wolpe, H., 1995, *The Post-secondary Education System: Towards Policy Formulation for Equality and Development*, EPU, UWC.

Barnard, R. and Farred, G., eds., 2004, 'After the Thrill is Gone: A Decade of Post-Apartheid South Africa', The South Atlantic Quarterly, Vol. 103, p. 4.

Bensimon, E. M., Neumann, A. and Birnbaum, 2001, 'Higher Education and Leadership Theory' in I.I.I. Jenniskens, ed., *Management and Decision-Making in Higher Education Institutions*, CHEPS and CHERI. pp. 279-291.

Bhana, S., 1977, 'The Racial Factor in Indian University Education', in H. van der Merwe and D. Welsh, eds., *The Future of the University in South Africa*, Claremont: David Philip.

Bond, P., 2004, 'South Africa Tackles Global Apartheid: Is the Reform Strategy Working?' in R. Barnard and G. Farred, eds., *After the Thrill is Gone: A Decade of Post-Apartheid South Africa, The South Atlantic Quarterly*, Vol. 103, No. 4

Bourdon, R., 1979, 'The 1970s in France: A Period of Student Retreat', *Higher Education*, Vol. 8, pp. 669 – 681.

Bourdieu, P. and Passeron, J., 1971, *Reproduction in Education, Society and Culture*, London: Sage Publications

Cele, G., Koen, C. and Mabizela, M., 2001, 'Student Politics and Higher Education in South Africa - Emerging Trends Since the Early 1990s', Paper presented at the EPU/ SRHE Conference on Globalisation and Higher Education. Cape Town.

Dahl, R. A., 1989, *Democracy and Its Critics*, New Haven and London: Yale University Press

Daniel, J., Southall, R. and Lutchman, J., eds., 2005, *State of the Nation: South Africa 2004-2005*: Pretoria, HSRC

Department of Education, 1997, *Education White Paper 3: A Programme for the Transformation of Higher Education*, (Pretoria).

Desai, A. and Pithouse, R., 2004, 'What Stank in the Past is the Present's Perfume: Dispossession, Resistance and Repression in Mandela Park', in R. Barnard and G. Farred, eds., *After the Thrill is Gone: A Decade of Post-Apartheid South Africa, The South Atlantic Quarterly*, Vol. 103, No. 4.

Gelb, S., 2005, 'An Overview of the South African Economy', in J. Daniel, R. Southall, and J.

Gwala, N., 1988, 'State Control, Student Politics and the Crisis in Black Universities,' in W. Cobbett and R. Cohen, eds., *Popular Struggles in South Africa*, London: James Currey.

Jordan, Z. P., 2005, 'Blood is Thicker than Water', available online at www.anc.org.za, accessed on the 27 June 2005

Johnson, B., 2000, 'Co-operative Governance? A Case Study of the Broad Transformation Forum at the University of the Western Cape', *Perspectives in Education*, Vol. 18, No. 3.

Kgware, W., 1977, 'The Role of Black Universities in South Africa" in H. van der Merwe, and D. Welsh, eds., *The Future of the University in South Africa*, Claremont: David Philip.

Koen, C., Cele, M. and Libhaber, A., 2005, 'Student Activism and Student Exclusions in South Africa', in *Journal of International Education and Development*.

Kulati, T., 2001, 'Leadership, Management and Institutional Change in South African Higher Education' Paper presented at the EPU/SRHE conference on Globalisation and Higher Education, Cape Town.
Maseko, S., 1994, 'Student Power, Action and Problems: A Case Study of UWC SRC, 1981-92', *Transformation*, Vol. 24, pp 25 - 45.
Ncayiyana, D. J. and Hayward, F. M., 1999, 'Effective Governance: A Guide for Council Members of Universities and Technikons', Centre for Higher Education and Training (CHET).
Nkomo, M. O., 1984, *Student Culture and Activism in Black South African Universities*, London, England: Greenwood Press,
Nzimande, B., 2004, 'Towards an Education System for Growth and Development: Assessing the Past Ten Years of Educational Transformation and Future Challenges from the Perspective of Parliament', Keynote address to the CEPD Conference on the Role of Education in First Decade of Democracy: A Critical Review. Braamfontein.
SACP, 2004, 'Political Report', Special National Congress, Ethekwini, April, available online at www.sacp.org.za, accessed on the 15 April 2004
SACP, 2004, 'Class Struggles in the National Democratic Revolution (NDR): The Political Economy of Transition in South Africa 1994-2004': A Central Committee Discussion Document, available online at www.sacp.org.za, accesses on the 11 February 2005.
SASCO, 1996 and 1997 Annual Congress Political Reports, available online at www.anc.org.za www.ilo.org.za
Wolpe, H., 1995, 'The Debate on University Transformation in South Africa: The Case of the University of the Western Cape', *Comparative Education*, Vol. 31, No. 2, pp 275-292

Interviews conducted

Interview with UWC SRC member, March 20, 2003
Interview with UCT SRC member, March 31, 2003
Interview with UDW academic member of Council, June 24, 2003
Interview with UWC SRC Member, March 23, 2003
Interview with UWC SRC member, March 23, 2003
Interview with UDW 1999/2000/2001 SRC Secretary General, June 24, 2003
Interview with DIT SRC Secretary General 2003
Interview with UDW ex SRC members (1997-2000), June 03, 2003
Interview with UWC SRC President, March 8, 2002
Interview with Cape Tech SRC President, May 8, 2002
Interview with Pentech Deputy President, September 23, 2002
Interview with Stellenbosch SRC January 31, 2002
Interview with UCT Registrar, February 26, 2002
Interview with UWC Registrar, December 11, 2001
Interview with Pentech Deputy Registrar, May 10, 2002
Interview with Cape Tech Deputy Vice Chancellor Student Affairs, April 16, 2002
Interview with UWC Institutional Planner, December 10, 2001
Interview with UWC Nehawu full-time shop steward, December 10, 2001
Interview with UWC Institutional Forum Chair, December 10, 2001
Interview with senior members of UWC Senate and Council, May 9, 2002

Interview with National Department of Education Official, February 14, 2002
Interview with UCT Student Development Officer, January 31, 2002
Interview with Cape Tech Student Development Officer, May 8, 2002
Interview with UWC Student Development Officer, February 18, 2002
Interview with UWC Chair of Committee Secretariat, December 10, 2001
Interview with UWC Vice Rector Student Affairs, December 12, 2002
Interview with University of Fort Hare SRC President, Student Services Officer, Treasurer General and SASCO Chairperson, September 4, 2003
Interview with University of Transkei SRC Deputy Finance Secretary, Deputy Social Welfare and Sport and Cultural Officer, September 5, 2003
Interview with Rhodes University ex-SRC Vice President 2002/2003 and 2003/4 SRC Chief Electoral Officer, September 3, 2003
Interview with Eastern Cape Technikon (Main Campus) SRC President, General Secretary, Chairperson (Queenstown branch), September 2, 2003
Interview with Rhodes University (East London Campus) SRC Secretary General, September 2, 2003
Interview with Border Technikon SRC Education and Transformation Officer, September 1, 2003
Interviews with UDW SRC President, Vice President and Information and Publicity Officer, June 24-27, 2003
Interview with Tswane University of Technology (Former TNG campus) SRC Deputy President and Gender officer Project Officer, March 29, 2004
Tswane University of Technology (former Pretoria Tech) SRC Secretary General- 30/03/04
UNISA National Deputy President Azasco and NSRC Projects and Finance Officer 30/03/04
Interview with Wits SRC President, March 31, 2004
Interview with Pretoria SRC President, April 1, 2004
Interview with UNISA National SRC Secretary General, April 1, 2004
Interview with UCM National PRO and UNISA local SRC secretary and UCM NEC member- project officer, April 1, 2004
Interview with UniZulu SRC Deputy President, April 5, 2004
Interview with Peninsula Technikon Deputy SRC President and SATSU President, July 7, 2003
Interview University of South Africa (Durban Campus) SRC member, June 25, 2003
Interview with 2002/3 Natal University SRC Faculty Officer (Durban Campus)

3. Zimbabwe

Higher Education and Student Politics in Zimbabwe

Annie Barbara Chikwanha

Introduction

This chapter analyzes the nature and role of student activism in Zimbabwe since 1980. As in many other countries, students in Zimbabwe have been at the forefront of the democratization debate and process since colonial rule. Since the early 1990s, they have become more organized to respond to societal demands and to demand good governance by forging alliances with other civic groups. Changes in the political and economic environment played a significant role in shaping these attitudes. After the long war for independence in the early 1980s, students rallied behind the government in the transformation phase and back then, most of their energy was directed towards community service. Towards the end of the 1980s, prescriptions of the economic structural adjustment programme had begun to affect the education sector and suspicions of the government's intentions towards the student body began to surface. By 1989, the one party state advocated by the government had become the pivotal point in student activism (Sithole 2001). Students felt the government was reneging on the democratic ideals fought for and this was a clear betrayal of the liberation struggle. The current government, led by architects of the armed struggle, hailed student activism during the struggle but in the post liberation war period, it has systematically denied students political space. This marginalization has compelled students in institutions of higher learning to organize and reclaim political space they had before (Melucci 1996). They therefore expressed their disenchantment through radical activism and did not accept their expected roles with a minimum of protest as the ruling party would have liked.

Throughout Zimbabwe's twenty-year democracy, students have functioned as an episodic oppositional force. They have periodically demonstrated against the government's policies which they view as violating their freedom and dignity. At times they demonstrated in solidarity with whichever group had grievances against the government but most of the time, they demand the improvement of their own conditions as students. This included constantly checking the environment so as to ensure their employment prospects. They in fact occupy significant political space and yet their ultimate aim appears to be the carving out of a desirable future for the university's educated.

Does this mean then that their rallying behind calls for change is merely instrumental? Could it be then that since one-party parliamentary 'democracy' works in clientelist networks, this compels students to constantly check their opportunities for mobility? What ideas of society and citizenship are implied in their activism? And how does religious belonging affect ideas about citizens or constructions about citizenship? Whilst an overview of the University of Zimbabwe's students' union and the Zimbabwe National Students' Union (Zinasu)[1] activities shed much light on the activities and orientations of the student body, it is important to note that this obscures those activities students participate in as individuals. The national students' union has shifted to become the fulcrum for most student activism in the country and behavioural cues for the student body seem to emanate from there.

The chapter starts off with a background briefing on the issues that have impacted significantly on student activism since 1980. The focus is on key events and legislation that are largely viewed as trigger points in student activism. This is followed by a brief description of the methodology employed in the study and an exposé of who the students are. This is done by seeking answers to the following questions: What is their background and how does it influence how they fit onto the intellectual social map? What are their aspirations as individuals? How do they intend to achieve their dreams? This is followed by a section on select forms of activism and it contains findings on student patterns of activism. The main issues addressed are: How is their activism defined? How do students deal with intra-student body tensions? How much space is there for female students to participate in student activities? and How has the government responded to student activism over time and space? The chapter concludes with a brief analysis of the implications of this activism on democratic governance. It is important to understand here what trigger points are in student activism since 1980.

Every group of student leaders in Zimbabwe has been arrested since 1989. The university has also been frequently closed by the university authorities and at times, those deemed to be disruptive were expelled. The longest shutdown of the university was in 1989 when the institution was closed for ten months as students resisted the University Amendment Act which came into effect in 1990.

The act was viewed all round as a clear attempt to curb academic freedom by breeding an educated patriotic class that was desired by the regime. The academic community was appalled as they thought the demise of the colonial regime would also be the end of all forms of repression, intellectual repression included. Unfortunately for Zimbabwe, the gagging of academics led to a loss of many bright lecturers who as immigrants, the government argued, should not have meddled in local politics. Shaddreck Gutto, a Kenyan law academic teaching at the university then, was amongst the casualtiess that were declared *persona-non grata*. Many lecturers were accused of fomenting student unrest. Student marches and demonstrations were violently disrupted but this did not stop students from devising all sorts of tactics to make their point. In some cases, they would assemble in the city in a bid to avoid the security blockages that were often placed around the city after the campus intelligence spies would have leaked the plans for a demonstration.

Towards the end of the 1980s, the University of Zimbabwe reacted very strongly to the one-party state agenda. Both students and lecturers led debates and meetings to discuss the one-party state and this became the order of life on and off campus. This was nothing new as in many other African countries, universities have been part of the various democratization struggles (Nyamnjoh and Nantang 2002). Whilst the government concentrated on control and order, neglect of academic standards became apparent as many PhDs left teaching to former teaching assistants. Likewise, many middle class parents who could afford to, began to send their children *en masse* to South African universities. The university slowly became an institution of higher learning for mostly the peasants and other low-income category earners.

In its short history after independence, the University of Zimbabwe has gone through five vice-chancellors in a period of twenty years. The president of the country, Robert Mugabe, assumed the overall position of chancellor of the university and later, when two other state universities were established, he also presided over all of them. This completed party/government control and hegemony over the direction of education and it also signaled the intolerance for diversity. With three state universities in different regions, the president as chancellor would, it was hoped by the ruling elite, symbolize the unity of the people and more importantly, of the future leaders. Naturally the confusion hampering effective and efficient governance was to replay itself in the universities as presidential appointees placed their loyalties elsewhere crucifying scholarship in the process. When Vice-Chancellor Walter Kamba resigned in 1990, he publicly cited the "the presence of many unprofessional fingers" in the running of the university. Through the Ministers of Higher Education, the universities soon became victims of the politics of exclusion. Here ethnic loyalties were superceded by liberation struggle loyalties as these ministers were often not from the ruling elite's clan but had to demonstrate their loyalty to the presidency's ideological preferences.

With such a background, it becomes important to understand what informs student activism in Zimbabwe and how attitudes to student and national politics have been formed over time.

Methodology

Semi-structured open-ended interviews were held with a wide range of students (across disciplines, gender, age, and year of study) for comparative material on how the students' struggles and how the political and economic strife in Zimbabwe contributed to the shaping of student activism. The leadership of the students' organizations (including former leaders) were interviewed for information on the organizations' goals and how these have changed over time. Selected student leaders were interviewed to get insight into their strategies and action orientations on different issues. Bearing in mind that not all students are actively involved in politics and other community-related activities, it was interesting to find out the background of those who participate. New data collected through a survey tapping into the students' attitudes, perceptions, fears and aspirations in relation to issues pertaining to governance, employment, leadership, wealth and the meaning of citizenship, makes it possible to test Mancur Olson's long standing hypothesis on collective action. Olson argues that members do not join interest groups in order to gain influence over government policy. Instead they are motivated to join by selective incentives.

The data was collected from two universities in different towns located in different provinces with different resource bases and different access to opportunities such as employment and mobility. The groups of students targeted for study were at Africa University in Mutare and at the University of Zimbabwe in Harare. All the students are organized into a national students' union, the Zimbabwe National Students' Union (ZINASU).[2]

This study took place during a very dark period in Zimbabwe's political history and the students were trapped right in the middle of the political tension. All universities were sharply divided into either ruling or opposition party enthusiasts - (at least publicly). Zimbabwe slid into anarchy in February 2000 after the public rejected the government's constitutional draft. White- owned land seizures by the war veterans of the liberation struggle did not spare the black community from the wrath of these state-backed marauding bands. A bloody post-election campaign left more than one hundred people dead after the 2000 parliamentary elections that saw a very new opposition party, the Movement for Democratic Change (MDC), scooping almost half of the seats. The new party had several Members of Parliament who had held leadership positions in the students' union at different times. This further heightened the tension and both the ruling party and the opposition competed hard to win converts amongst the student body. In a bid to hang on to power, the ruling party unleashed a reign of terror and many youths (unemployed) became involved in the white-owned farm invasions and these too accused students of sleeping with the enemy, the MDC. The hostile political and economic environment undoubtedly influenced the findings to some extent.

This study was delayed for some time because all public universities were closed for a long time after a spate of battles with the riot police and an indefinite strike by lecturers. Eventually the study was done when the institutions reopened but they were closed again within less than a month of reopening due to another lecturers' strike over cash flow problems. All these problems affected the originally planned methodology that was designed to target a larger sample at all four public universities in the country. As a result, only students at two universities were part of the study and other tertiary institutions were left out. The small sample, [n = 98], does not claim to be representative of the universe of students in higher institutions in Zimbabwe. Its main purpose was to reach a broader number of students that would enable the findings to be generalized to some extent. The sample was stratified by discipline of study, year of study, and gender (See Appendix A).

The sample had a good gender balance (51 per cent males/49 per cent females) even though the females at the university are still outnumbered by a ratio of almost 3:1. The point was to get the female voice on student activism, hence their deliberate oversampling. Most of the students in the sample were from the Social Science Faculty which is also the largest faculty at the University of Zimbabwe. The Education Faculty is equally large but because of the closure, it was difficult to get many students. The interviewed students were the ones who had stayed on at the two campuses on the weekend the questionnaires were administered. Generally, the sample reflects the populations of the different disciplines. The low figure for the first years (16 per cent) was due to the discontinuities caused by the switch over to the Western semester system in 2000 and reverting back to the old three-term system barely two years later.[3] The result was a delayed intake of first year students. Many of the students come from other regions outside of the two cities, Harare and Mutare, where the two universities are located, hence a large number still reside on the campuses. In the sample, 71 per cent stayed on the campus and 20 per cent lived with relatives. Only two per cent lived with their parents. Students are a religious lot as evidenced by the plethora of denominations on some campuses. The largest group belonged to Pentecostal churches (49 per cent), followed by the Roman Catholic Church at 27 per cent and the other Protestant churches, seven per cent. An almost equal proportion, (eight per cent did not belong to any church.

Who are the Students?

"...the voice of reason, of the nation, the canon of the quivering and the jealous defenders of peace, freedom and justice." Editorial comment, The College Times, December 2001

Being a student, which is a transitory stage (Baizerman and Magnuson 1996:1), creates space for a large segment of the youth population to experiment with various identities. Whilst this identity protects them from exploitation and abuse, it also exonerates them from onerous responsibilities. What then are the students' conceptions of themselves, of society and of the world? And more importantly, what is their perception of their role in the political and social space they have carved out for themselves? How do students define their role and what is their ultimate goal? What does being a student involve and what are the implications? What is their background (class, area of origin -- rural/urban) and What are their aspirations? Joel Barkan's (1975) study of students in the 1970s is important here as he asked questions back then that are still relevant today.

University students' possess knowledge that is of a higher standard and it opens access to many other opportunities. It is therefore normal for them to be status oriented. As a group with some status to preserve, Barkan (1975:129) argues that 'politics of self-interest' makes them challenge the state when their interests are directly threatened and support it when it suits them. Another argument is that students are constantly aware that they are institutionally powerless, therefore they need to always engage in new methods of struggle and new forms of organization to show their disenchantment. These inner contradictions are portrayed as a challenge by the ruling party/government hence hostilities and suspicions have largely determined the relationship between the two parties.

In many cases, students portray themselves as demoralized individuals who are constantly victimized by the government. They thus view themselves as victims of an unjust system whose purpose is to redress the nation's problem. At the same time, it is important to be cautious by acknowledging that studying does have a liberating and a liberalizing effect that does create space for the taking on of multiple identities. The absence of parental control gives students a chance for various forms of social experimentation with their personal and social identity. Could the activism we see then be simply an identity-pursuing project by the students? In Zimbabwe, the absence of an effective opposition left space that was filled in by the students (especially university) for a long time and they did translate many public concerns into action. The violation of human rights by the government has been one of their issues for a long time. However, as a privileged lot with access to information, it is amazing that their activism is not only largely political but also violent. What causes this violent disposition amongst the elite of the youths? Unemployed youths in the city capitalized on every public demonstration ever staged by the students forcing the government to step in and contain the demonstrations militarily.

Coping with the effects of the Economic Structural Adjustment Programme and the changing world has forced the students to become more organized to respond to societal demands and to demand good governance. Though most of their actions are directed against the government, for example when workers go on strike, denouncing corruption and human rights violations, they have at times taken sides with the government, confusing the public on what they actually stand for as when they demonstrated violently against the West and South Africa blaming them for Samora Machel's death in 1986.

Socio-economic Profile of the Students

The socio-economic background of university students in Zimbabwe has changed tremendously since independence. Up to 1980, the University of Zimbabwe was the only university in the country and it had a population of two thousand mostly white students from a middle class background. By the end of the 1980s, this population had increased five-fold following the increased access to secondary school education for blacks. White students withdrew from the university in droves in 1980-81 and went outside the country to finish off their degrees.[4] Whereas the colonial university had drawn its students from the middle and upper classes of the colonial society, the new government's policies opened up access to the peasant sector – a factor blamed for the political radicalism of the current crop of students.

The socio-economic background indicators relied on in this study are education and employment of parents, their occupation, and the last school attended before enrolling at the university. Employment of parents was crucial immediately after independence and after 1980. These two periods are important in that, in the immediate aftermath of independence, mainly children of prominent people were at the university with very few outstanding performers from the lower strata. By the end of the 1980s, many politicians and prominent people were again sending their children overseas to get more or less the same degrees they would get at the local university. During the same time period, only 28 per cent of the students were from subsistence farming households and by 1990 these had gone down to 17 per cent.[5] We can thus conclude that the same class background of students, from the black professional working class, continued to dominate the population at the university. As before, access to university was disproportionately in favour of children of civil servants and other public sector employees. In the sample, teachers were the largest occupational group among students' fathers.[6] The government grant and loan system could only accept surety from civil servants. Employment status of the parents does tell us a lot about access to university since only employed people qualified to guarantee the student loans. Students of unemployed parents had to seek a relative who would sign on behalf of the parents. Whilst this assured availability of funding, it also absolved the students of responsibility as the contracts did not bind them directly.

Twenty-two years later, almost one third of the students (31 per cent) at the universities in Zimbabwe still come from the professional group that is dominated by teachers *(see Table 1)*. The second largest group is the unskilled category (26 per cent) which again is dominated by civil servants since the police force, the army and prison warders are in that category. Their service makes it easy for them to guarantee the loans. At least 15 per cent of the students have parents who are skilled workers and another 14 per cent comes from a background of subsistence farming usually in the rural areas. A few commercial farmers, (seven per cent), send their children to the local university. The educational background of parents is more likely to influence the decision to help children through college since students from such a background have a better chance (resource wise) of getting to college. Again, the majority have parents who did not go through university themselves with about 15 per cent only of the sample having parents with degrees and again most of these were teachers. A significant percentage, 17 per cent, indicated that their parents had only had seven years of primary schooling. These factors all combine to present a profile of the average student at the university as coming from the working and peasant class family. It is also important to note that the parents, just like their children in college now, are also the same generation that endured the violence associated with the liberation struggle itself.

The issue of language is important in any analysis of the socio-economic background of university students because it very often is the first insignia of what the student is. It denotes everything about the students' background from the school they went to, where one's parents currently live, that is, whether it is a former white suburb or a black township, the ethnic group they belong to and what to expect from them in the event of a social relationship. With the majority of the students coming from rural areas and having attended 'rural' mission Group C and government Group B schools, many students spoke English with a heavy African accent and these were referred to as having Strong Rural Backgrounds (SRBs). The label is all encompassing of their traditional values, beliefs and decorum. These SRBs use their indigenous languages for communication both at home and socially. On the other hand are the 'nose brigades'. These are the ones who attended the government's Group A schools where English was the only acceptable medium of communication. Likewise, these students, mainly from the former white suburbs, spoke fluent English with a 'white accent' all the time even to communicate with their parents. Their mannerisms are equally reminiscent of television personalities and everything else that is modern and foreign. Nose brigades or 'salads'[7] as they later came to be known, hang out on their own, greet each other in English with affectionate hugs and can be easily singled out from their clothes (designer labels /hip-hop fashion) and gestures.

The school one attended before joining university is important in that it also tells a story about the background of the student. Many students from the working class (composed of teachers and nurses) attended mission schools that were established before independence. Since schools that offered advanced level studies were very few, it was easy to identify this professional working class and the business class by the schools the children went to.

Table 1: Socio-economic Background of the Students

Parents Occupation	%	Parents Education	%
Subsistence farmers	15	Primary school	17
Skilled workers	14	High school	35
Unskilled	26	Tertiary college	15
Professional (teachers, nurses)	31	Graduates	15
Unemployed	3	Refused to say	5
Self-employed	1	None	9
Retired	1	Don't know	2
Commercial farmer	7	Missing	2
Not applicable	2		
Home language	%		%
Shona	87	Mission	62
Ndebele	10	Government-Group A	7
English	1	Group B	30
Ndebele and Shona	1	Private	1
Shona and English	1		
Language mostly used with friends			
Shona	51		
English	19		
Ndebele and English	1		
Shona and English	29		
School attended			

After independence, the government restructured the education system and removed the colonial barriers at least in government schools and these came to be known as Group A and B schools. Nothing changed about the location or resource base of these schools. One would expect that the former white schools, the Group A, attracted all the students from privileged backgrounds (initially professional working class) who could afford to pay for the costly uniforms and compulsory sports gear (Bennell and Ncube 1994). School fees was controlled by the government which was also spending less on the Group A child. This is where the 'nose brigade' culture was bred and nourished. Up to 1981, all black students at the then only university came from about five government schools and the rest were from mission schools. By 1990, 40 per cent were coming from mission schools, 35 per cent from the Group B category and a modest 24 per cent from the Group A schools. Since entry requirements had not changed at the university, access was strictly on merit and the entire high school student body strove to meet the high qualifications. Access to elite schools was no longer essential to enter university.

At the time of the survey, mission schools were producing more students who qualified for university than the government schools. In the sample, 62 per cent had attended boarding mission schools, followed by 32 per cent who had been to the Group B government schools and lastly, seven per cent, only were from the former Group A schools where facilities are good but the quality of results is low. This is attributed mainly to the background of the children (nose brigades) who do not have the same zeal for education as do the disadvantaged Group B students. It is important to point out that students in the day government schools, the largest category countrywide, have never gone on strike to air their grievances on educational issues whereas all mission schools have been plagued by strikes and violent demonstrations since independence. It was also mission schools that led and participated in the anti-colonial struggles twenty-three years ago. Is it possible then that mission schools, most with 'missionary' ties overseas, have failed to transform themselves into democratic institutions that give students a voice? Does the university then become their outlet for the longed for freedom of expression?

Professional Aspirations

The realities of mobility that is prescribed by high academic qualifications drives the students to recognize the value of pursuing higher education. Almost the entire sample indicated that higher education is an important characteristic for getting where they want in their careers (98 per cent) (Table 2). That only 11 per cent find political careers as important implies an awareness of the devastating effects of the abuse of office and power by the current crop of politicians. Worse still, is the general lack of prosperity, expansion and sustenance of politically acquired wealth. Even though political office has been the main avenue for the current crop of indigenous entrepreneurs, a new spirit that shies away from the benefits of patronage/clientelism seems to be dominant in the student body. And contrary to what many observers state — that the entrepreneurship spirit is missing in Africa — a very high percentage of the respondents (87 per cent) did express a desire to run their own business empires.

Unfortunately, the same cannot be said about community leadership which has lost its luster, with only 27 per cent stressing its importance. Though community was not defined in the questionnaire, it was assumed that the concept was applied to the wider social organizations outside of the family that were not profit-oriented. In this sense, it would cross over into political boundaries. However, individual success does matter more than the service and upliftment of a community. More students appear to have 'Messianic' tendencies as portrayed by the world of Non-Governmental Organizations (NGO). NGOs provide increased opportunities to access foreign currency, international travel and exposure. The last two are some of the most desirable pecks that drive these desires. The question is: Could the 'Messianic' tendencies be more dominant than the desire to join the lucrative private sector? The private sector very often provides career channels unlike the NGO world where jobs do not necessarily lead to careers. However, students tend to find the realities of the 4X4 wheel drive NGO world more appealing. After all, NGOs are slowly catching up with the private sector in terms of their numbers and diversity that still, amazingly enough, address more or less similar issues.

Table 2: Important Characteristics for a Successful Future %: How important are the following characteristics for your success in future?

Acquire higher education	98
Career in politics	11
Career in private business sector	60
In the NGO sector	78
Becoming successful in a personal business	87
Becoming a community leader	27

There is a good match between the students' likely professions and the characteristics they require for the careers. Most of those studying in the professional qualifications sector, (38 per cent), indicated that they would like to work in the private sector except for the four per cent who were more realistic and indicated that their chances of working as lawyers for the government were better

(*Table 3*). A large percentage, (24 per cent), are more likely to work as teachers and this is more so with students from Africa University and the Arts students who are not necessarily trained to fit into general employment categories as they are offered very academic courses only. The university is seriously lagging behind in terms of training students for the information and technology sector. With the whole government still running on a manual basis, coupled with the spiraling economy and government attempts to stifle the growth of the communication industry,[8] it is no wonder that many students do not seem to realise the opportunities that lie in this sector.

The administrative positions that eight per cent of the respondents prefer raise queries on the actual value of the qualifications the students are getting. On the other hand, it could be a warning against degrees that do not have a clear target out there and yet there are also areas out there that call for specific skills. Other than the Business Administration degree, the universities do not offer general management courses except for the elitist and expensive Masters in Business Administration programme for working professionals only. Likewise, the Masters in Public Administration course only takes about fifteen students a year and this includes those directly from undergraduate classes. The any job category, mentioned by 10 per cent, fits the sometimes stereotyped erratic behaviour of the youth who will simply go with the tide because it is expected of them to do so. However, in Africa, the reality is that many students have to figure out what they intend to do before they leave university but even then, the job market has been stagnant for some decades making it difficult to secure employment in the desired areas. This prompts many to leave for the diaspora.

Table 3: Professional Aspirations %: With your educational background, what job are you likely to secure upon your graduation?

Teaching	24
IT industry	3
NGOs	4
Professional-private sector [accountants, lawyers, engineers]	38
Administrative positions	8
Any job	10
Don't know	2
Public service	4

How likely is it that students will realize their career hopes? The question: *What do you think about your prospects of becoming successful in the areas you said are important to you?* was posed to the interviewees. Just over half of the respondents,(53 per cent), are very confident that they can realize their aspirations and the other 42 per cent think they are likely to be successful as well. Many students tend to take up other professional studies such as accounting, personnel management and marketing with other private institutions outside of the university. They then use credits already acquired from the university to skip some of the modules in these professional courses and earn themselves qualifications that make up for the 'deficit of experience' demanded by the business world. Whilst this can be applauded, it also is evidence of the abundant time on their hands. This is a reason sometimes used by politicians to explain their meddling in national politics.

Most of the students,(48 per cent), plan to secure jobs in the near future and the presumption is that this will be in the country *(Table 4)*. Almost ten per cent of the respondents intend to leave the country to pursue higher education. Another 31 per cent indicated that they intend to leave the country in search of work bringing the total of those who want to leave after their studies to 40 per cent. And an almost similar percentage,(nine per cent), indicated that they intend to pursue higher education - probably in the country as this was not specified. More social science students intend to pursue further studies than from any other discipline (32 per cent). Most lawyers pointed to the intention to secure jobs locally and the largest category intending to seek employment outside the country are the education students at 60 per cent. Fuelled by the current British recruitment exercise for teachers and nursing professionals and the economic problems that are mostly a result of bad governance, many educated Zimbabweans have left the country since 2000. This leaves the universities with the role of developing human capital that will not realize its full potential since those that leave the country with high academic qualifications will only qualify for menial tasks in the West.

Table 4: Future Plans and Prospects %: What are you plans after you finish your training/degree?

Get a job	48
Pursue a higher degree	9
Leave the country for further studies	9
Leave the country to seek employment	31
Missing	4

History of Student Activism

The Students' Union at the university has been a tool of political socialization since the mid-1980s. Many of the current political leaders were all active in the union and some students who aspire for political office still learn the tricks of the trade in the union. Of late, the students' slogan has become, "change the world". Students explain their activism as a revolution within a revolution that addresses the injustice in the society. It is important to point out that students were socialized into a culture of violent demonstrations that has been institutionalized over time by their predecessors. Violence is more of a trademark of the organization but it is clearly not the dominant action.[9] The nature of political socialization and the political culture in Zimbabwe are such that violence is perceived and accepted as the only language understood by authorities and opponents alike.

To get more insight into the nature and factors related to student activism, a series of questions required answers and these are: What are the students' ideas of a just society? What is the nature of their social and political activism? How do state institutions and civic organizations respond to their demands? How much space exists for them in these institutions to shape policies that affect them and To what extent do global influences orient their activism? In a previous research exercise, several students remarked that, because they were educated, it was their right to lead other 'youths out there who need to be led'.[10] The assumption was that only knowledge acquired from distinct institutions (universities) allowed people to lead others. With such an openly arrogant world-view, we are right then to ask: Does the student body then provide effective guidance to youth public action?

A number of factors were identified as having an impact on student activism in this study and what is presented here is not an exhaustive list. The factors are religion, discipline of study, year of study, gender and residential status of the student. With many of the student belonging to Pentecostal churches that openly call for disengagements from unreligiously fulfilling activities, it is assumed that those who consider religion to be of fundamental importance would not be active in politically-related issues. When we turn to the discipline factor, we look at the tensions caused by the different types of knowledge. For a long time, there has been some tension between the hard sciences and the soft sciences as students from the former discipline often ignore calls to boycott classes with the rest of the students. There is a general attitude that they feel superior and they therefore attempt to detach themselves from the main students' union activities. First year students are blamed for most of the violence that occurs during student demonstrations and likewise third year students are blamed for planning demonstrations in order to disrupt examinations because they will not be ready for them. Though this cannot be tested in this paper, it will be possible to analyze the nature and level of activism by year of study. Also we expect male students to be more active in student politics as most of the activities require the ability to engage in running battles with the riot police. Finally, students resident on campus have always been blamed for the radical activism within the student body. What this survey sought to find out was the general pattern of activism without necessarily accounting for the violence.

Religion and Activism

Student politics in Zimbabwe has been dogged by religious tensions since 2000. For example, when the multi-denominational 2001 students' union office bearers assumed office, they were a solid diverse group that seemed fit for executive duties.[11] However, within a short time, the camp had been split into several camps, the Christians (Pentecostals) and the Comrades, the Christ-like and the cadres (to use their lingo). The cadre group accuses the Christ-like for criticizing their radicalism and using heavenly logic to interpret situations that needed practical earthly reasoning. The Christian groups on campus openly throw their weight behind preferred candidates, usually known Christians, such that voting takes place not only on disciplinary and ethnic lines, but religious ones as well. These problems led to the establishment of a student Electoral Supervisory Commission to oversee student elections together with independent observers from Zinasu, the umbrella student organization. The question that arose immediately was: who monitors the umbrella body (Zinasu's) elections? This signaled mistrust within the students' union.

To find out the impact of religion on student activism, the question: *How important is your religion to you?* was posed to the respondents. Almost all the students reported that religion was important to them. Responses were rated on a four-point scale from 'essential', 'very important', 'omewhat important' to 'not important'.

The Pentecostal students are just as active as the Protestant[12] students and whereas there are points of convergence, there are also differences in the areas of emphasis. The most vibrant group are the Catholics who have several support organizations linked to the University of Zimbabwe structures. There is strong mobilization by the leaders of the Catholic organizations to encourage students to have their spiritual and social needs met through church related associational activities. This is also an attempt to detract them from reckless sexual behaviour. With regard to other activities, the Protestants are generally in the lead. Pentecostal activism is at its lowest in students' union politics (six per cent and voting in student elections (39 per cent) but highest in national elections (92 per cent) (Table 5). Even Protestant participation is low in student politics at 30 per cent. Though the two groups report high levels of membership in organizations, it is important to note that this is both in one area, religious organizations. The difference is that with the Catholic religious organizations, political debates are always part of the agenda.

Table 5: Activism by Type of Church %

Nature of Activity	Pentecostal	Protestants & Catholics	None	Others
Participation in demo/ strike off/on campus	52	86	75	75
Attended community/ studentMeeting	46	53	63	50
Participation in student union Politics 8	30	63	25	
Voluntary service	63	57	38	25
Active member of an organization	84	86	50	25
Voting in students union Election	39	52	75	50
Voting in National Election	92	88	75	50

The non-denominational students are the most active category in student politics at 63 per cent and voting in student elections 75 per cent. They are also less likely to engage in voluntary activity (38 per cent). Overall, religious students' participation in political student affairs is on the low side and the 'cadres' (the none category) appear to be in the lead hence their being pointed out as the ones steering student activism along the violent path. Participation in religious groups is also a form of escape from the temptations of the secular world. The desire to be saved from drugs, alcohol and Aids spurs many youths to join religious groups. Zimbabwe's economic problems have also compelled the youth to turn to divine intervention in their quest for a prosperous future (Osei-Hwedie 1989).

Table 6 : Frequency of Activism by Different Variables %:

Activity	Total		Religious Essential	Residence* On Off		Yr of Study	Males		Fem	
Participation in demo/ strike off/on campus	64	28	61	61	75	79	66	35	63	22
Attended community/ Student meeting	48	47	49	46	50	58	58	51	38	43
Participation in student union politics	17	-	9	14	30	18	28			6
Voluntary service	57	30	53	59	50	55	58	24	57	36
Active member of an organization	82	63	90	49	45	82	88	59	76	67
Voting in students union election	50	60	43	49	45	67	66	41	33	40
Voting in national election	90	33	88	87	95	94	84	37	96	30

Notes: Residence Column: Reported percentages are of those who answered yes
*First figure is of those staying on campus and the second is of those staying with relatives[13]

Generally, associational membership,(82 per cent), and participation in national elections, (90 per cent), are both very high within the student body *(Table 6)*. However, these are at their lowest in student union politics where only 17 per cent reported participation in student union politics, attending student meetings (48 per cent) and voting in student elections (50 per cent). Dissatisfaction with the way the students' union is run has led to this disenchantment and rather than confront their union leaders, the student body simply chooses to withdraw. Active membership was highest in religious organizations (58 per cent), followed by social organizations (12 per cent), in political organizations ten per cent and lastly, sports at four per cent. The 90 per cent who say that religion is very essential are active members of some organizations with most of them participating actively in religious organizations (63 per cent) and the other 17 per cent in social organizations. Amongst the female respondents, no-one reported being a member of a political organisation and the paltry 10 per cent of the claims were made by males. More than half the females, (54 per cent), reported membership in religious organizations with even more males (61 per cent) being members of religious organizations. Engineering students are the least active in religious organizations (17 per cent) and the second least active are law students (31 per cent).

The most active in this realm are the usually more mature education students (80 per cent) and those studying agriculture (73 per cent). The law students are the most active in the political realm (27 per cent). This is confirmed by the fact that many of the most revered student leaders came from this faculty and some have moved on to prominent positions in the political arena.

Religiosity, as indicated by the frequency of church attendance, is high in both sexes with 60 per cent of the females attending church daily compared to 18 per cent of the males. Another 27 per cent attend at least two to three times a week compared to 44 per cent of the males who do so. Those staying on campus attend daily (27 per cent) as do the ten per cent who stay with relatives. Attendance patterns are similar between Pentecostals and Catholics with around 30 per cent reporting daily attendance. Time devoted to church certainly does compete with time that would be spent on other activities. Campus life allows the students to make almost all decisions without consulting anyone and there are no parental restrictions to control the movement and associational habits of students. As a result, many of them have plenty of time to invest in other activities. Students staying on campus and with relatives are generally more active than those staying with parents and alone as lodgers. They are also more likely to participate in student politics, demonstrations and voting in elections.

Table 7: Activism by Type of School Attended Prior to Going to University

Activity	Group A%	Group B%	Group C%
Participation in demo/strikeoff/ on campus	29	69	67
Attended community/student meeting	57	45	48
Participation in student union Politics	14	7	23
Voluntary service	43	62	56
Active member of an organization	71	68	87
Voting in students union election	43	38	57
Voting in national election	57	90	93

Former group A students are the least active in activities that are likely to escalate into violence such as demonstrations (29 per cent) and more than two thirds of those from mission and group B schools reported participating in demonstrations *(Table 7)*. Attendance of student community meetings as well as participation in student politics is on the low side throughout with the group A lot participating more in this area. In line with the 'salad culture' which emphasizes entertainment and hanging out in classy recreational centres, former group A students are active members in two types of organizations only, social and religious groups even though the figure of those reporting overall active membership is high at 71 per cent. Former mission students are the most active members across all organizations at (87 per cent) and they are also the only ones who report membership in political organizations (eight per cent). Again, the former group B students revealed that they are just as active as the former group A students in students' politics at 68 per cent. The former mission students report the highest levels of participation in students' union politics (23 per cent), membership in organizations (87 per cent) and voting in student elections (57 per cent). This indicates that much of the participation is spontaneous for many of the students.

It is essential to note that student activism at universities in Zimbabwe is largely viewed as a male domain mainly because the leadership is almost always exclusively male and the demonstrations the public sees all the time are always carried out mostly by the male students. Gender is a very crucial division with women facing constraints that are imposed partly by tradition. The females internalize these constrains but they also tend to specialize in different forms of participation that focus more on informal community based activities. Their participation thus becomes geared to fulfilling basic needs as shown by their opposition to violence. The male students argue that gender is never an issue as females rarely run for student affairs' leadership positions. In the few cases when they have done so, it was not clear whether it was other girls who had mainly voted for them.

The females are unhappy with the conduct of their male students whom they accuse of resorting to violence unnecessarily to seek attention. They argue that the violence, the inflammatory and vitriolic foul language used by the militant members of the union keeps them out. When compared to males, female activism is rather low in most of the activities except in voting in national elections where 96 per cent reported participation and membership in organizations where just over three quarters reported being members. Its important to emphasize that 55 per cent of this membership is in religious organizations. Their compassionate nature shows when it comes to voluntary service where they almost match their male counterparts. Females do not participate in the students' politics but they do vote during union elections (33 per cent) even though this is only half of the male population that votes (66 per cent). When females participated in demonstrations, the main reason given for their participation was exactly the same as that given by the males: demanding a new constitution and the demand for a corruption-free nation.

The only time female students initiated and staged a demonstration was in solidarity with thirty-six other girls who had been kicked out of university residence by a female warden for entertaining males after hours. The event was triggered by the eviction of a fourth-year law student who had kept a male visitor in her room after the stipulated hours. This was in fact a colleague with whom she was working with on a project and as it was raining, he was waiting for the rain to stop before walking over to the male hostel. After her eviction following what the students called a 'kangaroo court', the girls camped in the foyer until she was reinstated. The next morning they staged a mini-demonstration outside the warden's house where they chanted and sang revolutionary songs. They alleged that wardens and hall committee members were ruthless and arbitrary in their treatment of students. Hundreds of male students converged to watch this rare phenomenon and within a few hours, they had hijacked the demonstration and all other issues such as low grants and loans and corruption were pushed to the fore-front. The police were later called in to disperse the very large crowd that had turned rowdy.

Electoral Participation

Despite the students' rhetoric about good governance and respect for human rights, students do not participate in elections, as responsible citizens should. Only 19 per cent are aware of this obligation as citizens (*Table 8*). That as many as 52 per cent state that they do not feel anything could imply the deliberate choice to ignore peaceful means of effecting change. Or that they are simply stating that 'all politicians are the same.' Hence the foregone conclusion that students are simply interested in violence because of the anarchy it creates for other opportunities. However, if apathy is the unconscious recognition students make of the fact that they are powerless, then withdrawal from the process may also signify powerlessness. In this case, many students reported voting in national elections and the question is, why is this so? Some revealed honestly in the face-to-face interviews that they simply enjoyed the frenzy caused by the campaigning during election times. Hence they just got caught up in the heat of the moment.

Table 8 : Voting Behaviour %: Which one of the following statements best describes your feelings about voting in an election?

I get a feeling of satisfaction out of it	15
I vote only because it is my duty to do so	19
I feel annoyed, voting is a waste of time	10
I do not feel anything in particular	52
Don't know	36

Political Interest and Knowledge

To measure political interest we posed the question: *How much discussion about matters of government and politics is there at the university you attend?* and *How often do you participate in these discussions?* Though the majority (57 per cent) agree that there is a great deal of discussion at their university, very few (29 per cent) reported that they participated in these discussions *(Table 9)*. Of these, only 13 per cent participate at least two to three times a week and another nine per cent reported participating once a month. Almost two thirds believe that they can exert a great deal of influence on the government with another 26 per cent agreeing that they can exert some influence. The largest category of 65 per cent who rarely participate in political discussions voted in national elections and again the 68 per cent who rarely participate believe that they can exert a great deal of influence on the government. This implies that students are somehow interested in deliberative democracy. Still, the question points to the preference of confrontational means for solving disagreements. It gives pointers to the lack of tolerance they accuse the government of. And perhaps, it raises questions on the link between political interest and voting behaviour?

Table 9 : Voting and Political Interest %: How often do you participate in these discussions? How much influence can students like yourself exert on the government of this country today? (% reporting a great deal)

Attendance	Voted national Election	(Yes) Great Influence
2 or 3 times a week	14	13
Once a week	6	8
Once a fortnight	2	2
Once a month	9	7
I rarely participate	65	68
I never participate	5	3

Views on Governance

Students are divided on the question that they are not willing to stand up in defence of democracy (49 per cent on both the negative and positive sides-Table 10). This apparent division has probably contributed to the marginalization of their contributions and lamentations on issues of national significance. On their own as a student body, they do not get an audience with state agents and this has pushed them towards forging alliances with other civic organizations including political organizations. This is a stance that has angered the government as they are seen as cavorting with the enemy. An interesting issue is their view on government by an educated elite. This question comes about because the main contender for the presidency in the 2000 national elections was a former workers' union leader who does not have university education. The ruling party campaign focused on this as his second weakness since the argument is that international economics and relations are beyond his grasp as a high school graduate. This issue has left the nation bordering on skepticism as time and again they are made to question his adequacy as a presidential candidate. In the responses, 62 per cent agreed/strongly agreed that the best form of government is that run by the educated and 35 per cent felt that this was not necessarily true. More positively, a large percentage demonstrated their support for democracy when they disagreed with the statement that speech must be curtailed in the interests of state security and good government (76 per cent) but still there are traces of a significant proportion that sanctions despotic tendencies. The contradiction arises on the question that government must act in the best interests of the people even though it may not be what they want. Here almost all the students agreed with this view (92 per cent). Though this may contradict their views *vis-à-vis* upholding other freedoms, it supports their arrogant stance as revealed in interviews that they, as the educated elite of the youth, must lead the other youths out there.

Table 10 : Views on Governance %

	Ltd freedom of speech	Gov't run by educated	Defence of freedom	Gov't must act for people
Strongly agree	1	6	14	86
Agree	19	56	35	6
Disagree	59	28	37	2
Strongly disagree	17	7	12	3
Missing	3	3	2	2

1st column responses to question: Freedom of speech must be limited in the interests of security and good government

2nd column responses: The best form of government is that run by those who are most educated

3rd column responses Most students at my university do not have the courage to stand up and fight for what they believe in

4th column responses The government of a country should do what is best for the people even though it may not be what they want

The Paradox of Student Leadership

Students are generally dissatisfied with their leadership. Performance of the students' union leadership over the years has left them alienated from the student body. Only 14 per cent expressed satisfaction with the leadership and another 23 per cent felt it represented their interests. With such low levels of confidence, it is clear that the student leadership lacks legitimacy. The student leadership has devastated resources of the union, paralyzing all other activities. The students' greatest asset is their intellectual talents but the absence of institutional support for their potential creativity hampers their development. The little support they get is from human rights groups and what they call 'counter insurgency groups' that are against the government. Their only physical asset, the Students' Union building that was donated by the British government in the-mid 1980s, has psychological significance as they feel that they belong there. It demarcates the boundary between them and the university authorities as well as the rest of the world they interact with. They withdraw to this place when they plan demonstrations and eavesdroppers are not tolerated. Space in this building is rented out to the public and the rentals are used to run the union. Elected leaders collect money for all students'-union-related business and are accused of spending it all on their salaries and perks. There are allegations of corruption and cronyism in the union, and the electoral process is divided along political parties and tribal lines. Students thus feel that they do not gain anything from being union-paying members.

To legitimize its existence, the union leadership has thus assumed a heavy human rights bias at the expense of general student welfare. Ethnic factionalism too has affected the student body with the minority Ndebele students being forced to create their own public space in their region. After failing to secure the post of secretary general in the union, a former student leader was told frankly, 'No matter how good you are, you are never voted into top office because you are Ndebele. You failed to make the Student Representative Council (SRC) presidency because you are Ndebele.'[14] The Matebeleland[15] Development Society, a Ndebele-led organization, sponsored his campaign which worsened the situation. Another eloquent, charismatic and proud student leader failed to be SRC president because he was taken to be more Ndebele than he is Shona. His father is Shona, the mother is Ndebele but he grew up in Matebeleland therefore he was seen as Ndebele. Another rival in the campaign used this in his campaign and convinced the student body not to accept him. Colleagues told him, 'We cannot vote for you because you are Ndebele.' Like the ruling politicians, the students do not want anyone from Matebeleland to be involved in student politics. For the Shonas, their superiority is also in numbers at the campus and in that the ethnic group rules the country. For the Ndebeles, their pride is in their strong cultural heritage and they call their region the home of kings. Socially, there is a lukewarm relationship between the two tribes and perhaps a former secretary general of the SRC portrayed these tribal tensions when he stated, 'I am tribal conscious, not a tribalist.' Tribal politics in the students' union does take the same character as national politics.

The administration too is accused of discriminating against Ndebele students and even the ministers of education have been known to accord audience to Shona student leaders only. Even the riot police are known to punish Ndebeles more severely than other students. In one incident during a demonstration that had turned into a riot police invasion, a Ndebele student pleaded for mercy with a policeman in his Ndebele language and another policeman retorted, 'Rova mwana waNyongolo uyo, imbwa iyo!' *(Beat Nyongolo's relative, beat the dog!).*[16] At the social level, Ndebele boys often date Shona girls and such relationships are held in contempt by the male Shona students. The relationships are under a lot of pressure hence they do not last very long. The Shona girls also revealed parental prejudices that fuel this hostility. Many pointed out that they are cautioned at home not to date Ndebele guys as they are prone to violence.

Most Important Problems – The Students' Agenda

In a bid to understand the restless nature of students in the country, students were asked to rank four problems that had been identified earlier on in in-depth interviews as explaining all the violent demonstrations on campus. These are finance, the curriculum — irrespective of discipline, housing and security. The respondents were asked to rank these in order of priority and all mentioned finance as the most important issue, followed by housing (89 per cent) security came in third and the curriculum came in last. In 1998, there was a violent demonstration against diminishing services at the university. Bayart's (1993) 'Politics of the belly' began to dominate from then on, but still students write petitions on other issues such as improving the library and increasing investment in education. They still do not seem to be concerned with the curriculum and its relevance to the nation's circumstances and industrial needs. Petitions on curriculum-related issues are written at the departmental level usually by disgruntled students. Demands are expressed directly to the government officials responsible for higher education. The problem is that when they fail to vent their anger on university authorities, the students turn on college property and destroy everything in their way. Their priority then is to discuss hunger and their 'poverty'. Like the general Zimbabwean indigenous public, students too have a 'subsistence culture' that is exhibited in excessive and unaffordable expenditure on clothes. This subsistence culture is defined by Masunungure (2004) as action that is oriented towards the consumption of whatever there is to consume — large or small.

From 1980, all students, irrespective of need, received financial support from government in the form of a grant and loan scheme. This was an incentive to all students to join the education band-wagon even if they could afford to pay. Up to 1993, the government had never demanded that students should pay back the loans they received so that others could also benefit from what was initially designed to be a revolving fund. The best part of the financing system was the 'grant' which was part of the package intended to support the students' personal and academic needs. This of course was pocket money and it was treated as such by all students. Even those who were resident on campus with all expenses paid for failed to channel this money towards purchasing of books. The grant pay-out was usually received about two weeks after classes started and for another week, students would continue to miss classes as they celebrated their good fortune. To legitimize missing classes, it became common for demonstrations to be planned to coincide with pay-out dates. Unfortunately, the privatization of student services in 1999 eroded the power of the pay-out tremendously as students had to provide their own food in addition to the usual extras. This slight discomfort did not last for a long time as the government completely withdrew the grant and loans and commercialized the loans in 2001. Since then, the frequency of demonstrations has increased to one every six weeks whenever the university is open.

What Values Drive the Students?

African cultures have been said to emphasize the communal good over individual destiny, leading people to think and act as passive, differential and dependant clients of external forces rather than as active agents with some degree of control over their own lives or the wider polity (Mattes and Bratton 2003:7). The findings from this study provide contradictory evidence as African students have demonstrated that whilst they do not necessarily lack a sense of responsibility, they certainly do not conform to the expectations of those in authority and are not scared to take risks necessary to effect democratic governance. This is evidenced by their participation in demonstrations discussed earlier on. But still society's views still count in their value system.

To gauge their value orientations, the following question was asked: *Which of the following would you say determines what your family members and the people in your area think of you? (a) your superior education (b) your participation in helping them and (c) your future economic success?* A very high percentage of the students,(83 per cent), reported that they enjoy a very high social status and prestige amongst their family and community members even though an almost non-existent job market probably dampens their spirits. There is a general feeling that university graduates are more respected in society (94 per cent). It is therefore logical to conclude that influence from family and one's community, no matter how subtle, does have an important effect on persistence by the student's natural desire to uphold that image. However, a significantly large percentage has come to realize that university graduates do not necessarily make more money (64 per cent). Again not all of them believe that graduates get the best jobs available. One important question to ask is: Do students feel they have the power to change their lives?

Students from all disciplines are proud of their national identity (all above 83 per cent) with medical students being the least proud (50 per cent). Education and law students both (over 95 per cent) agree that Zimbabwe is a great country signaling the opportunities that exist for them after they leave college. Almost all the respondents,(95 per cent), expressed strong attachments to their country which contradicts their earlier stance in which as many as 40 per cent indicated their plans to leave the country after their studies. In disciplines where jobs are harder to find, a large percentage feel they have no power to change their life (Social Science 33 per cent and Arts 20 per cent). Still, Medical and agricultural students rate themselves as having very few rights (both over 68 per cent).

When it comes to the religious divide, Pentecostals feel slightly less powerful at 28 per cent when compared to the Protestants at 33 per cent and none of the females felt they had all the rights and neither did they feel they were very powerful. As can be expected in a patriarchal society, more males (30 per cent) reported having greater control over decisions affecting their everyday activities with only eight per cent of the females saying the same. Male students (14 per cent) feel they have most rights and that they are mostly powerful. Female students are less confident than the males with twice as many rating themselves as totally powerless to change their lives. Those residing on campus feel very powerful with all rights (52 per cent), as do all the lodgers. While those staying with parents all reported that they had 'some control over some decisions', lodgers reported having full control over most decisions. More females reported being somewhat happy (68 per cent) when compared to males (40 per cent) and Social Science students are the happiest lot at 26 per cent followed by Agriculture (18 per cent) and Engineering (17 per cent). Those staying alone as lodgers and on campus are all very happy with both groups reporting a record 100 per cent. All those residing with parents reported being somewhat happy (13 per cent). By discipline, the group that struggles the most to get jobs, Arts, are the unhappiest (15 per cent). Most sit on the fence (ranging from 20 to 35 per cent) across all the faculties.

Conclusion

Student activism in Zimbabwe appears to be driven by a combination of factors: historical factors (religion, high school background and ethnicity), gender, the political environment, future aspirations and global influences. Whereas traditional, mainstream religions such as Catholicism tend to instil values that lead to civic engagement, the new Pentecostal wave tends to encourage withdrawal from broader public association. This results in members harbouring a parochial mindset with regard to the exercise and duties of responsible citizens. In the same vein, older schools such as mission schools, produce students who are more likely to question governance and democratic issues as opposed to the recently opened up former white schools that had enjoyed peace and stability during the independence struggle.

On entering a restrictive and authoritarian political environment, students who have wrestled with traditional and conservative religious and educational authorities are more likely to demand justice and insist on being heard. They have grown to harbour values that orient their activism in favour of desirable change. However, the absence of the female student in active engagement in public space is a cause for concern as their needs fail to get on the agenda of policy makers. Their continued concern for involvement in compassionate activities can and should be applauded, but it also merits attention in that transference of compassionate to political affairs could instil some pacifist tendencies in the students who believe in the use of violence to get attention.

Appendix A

Table 1. : Characteristics of the Zimbabwe Sample

Gender	%	Residence	%
Males	51	Campus	71
Females	49	With parents	20
Discipline		With relatives	
		Lodgers	1
Discipline		Year of study	
SocialSciences	24	First	
Natural Sciences		Second	37
Arts	13	Third	33
Education	5	Fourth	12
Law	11	Fifth	1
Medicine	4	Other	-
Agriculture	11		
Engineering	6		
Other	0		
Age		Religious	
Below 20	1	Denomination	
20-23	38	Catholic	27
24-27	5	Pentecostal	49
over 27		Protestant	7
		None	4
		Other	

N=98

Notes

1. ZINASU is a student initiative that came about to address national issues of access to education, governance, human rights and health. The union is made up of all students who are members of the students' union at the different tertiary institutions. The privatization of student services has re-introduced the bottleneck system (reminiscent of colonialism) as it is only the rich who can afford education now. The group lobbies for access to education through parliament and claims non-partisanship.
2. Most degree programmes at the universities take three years to complete except for agriculture, engineering and medicine.
3. The white students exodus was partly a response to the reorientation of university education advocated by the government and partly in anticipation of the inevitable fall in standards.
4. By 1985, over 40 per cent of the students' fathers were teachers. The figure rose from 25 per cent in 1980-81. Bennell and Ncube (1994) carried out a study on the socio-economic background of African University Students in Zimbabwe since independence. They used students' records to extract data on randomly selected students from four of the ten faculties at the university.
5. Nose-brigades are also called salads to denote their food preferences. Salad eating is in this sense, usually associated with dieting and balancing the diet.
6. In 2001, the government made it mandatory for all internet providers to submit all records of email correspondence by public to the government security agents. This was aimed at curbing the communication channels of the opposition party, MDC, which had established a wide network with citizens living in the diaspora.
7. Interview with former SRC president.
8. Interview with SRC member.
9. Interview with former SRC official.
10. The Protestant group is composed of the mainstream churches such as Lutheran, Methodist and Anglicans. However, in this particular table, they were added together with the Catholics.
11. Interview with former SRC secretary general.
12. Matebeleland is one of the provinces in the southern part of Zimbabwe. It is inhabited mostly by Ndebele-speaking people who fled from Tshaka Zulu's Mfecane wars in the 18th century. Ndebeles are the second largest language group in Zimbabwe after the Shonas. They have been systematically excluded from office and power since 1980.
13. Nyongolo was the name of the late vice president, Joshua Nkomo, who led the opposition party, ZAPU during the first 9 years of independence before the party united with the ruling ZANU-PF party.

References

Baizerman, M. and Magnuson D., 1996, 'Do We still Need Youth as a Social Stage?' Available online at http:/www.alli.fi/nyri/young/1996-:/www.alli.fi/nyri/young/1996-3artikkelBaizerman 3-96.htm.

Barkan, J., 1975, *An African Dilemma*, Oxford University Press.

Bayart, J. F., 1993, *The State in Africa: the Politics of the Belly*, UK: Longman.

Bennell, P. and Ncube, M., 1994, *The Socio-economic Background of African University Students in Zimbabwe Since Independence*, University of Zimbabwe.

Masipula, S., 2001, 'Fighting Authoritarianism in Zimbabwe', in *Journal of Democracy*, 12, pp. 160-169.

Masunungure, E., 2004, 'Towards Understanding Some Obstacles to Professionalism in Africa: A view Through Contextual Lenses' in F., Appiah, D., Chimanikire and T. Gran, eds., *Professionalism and Good Governance in Africa*, Copenhagen Business Press.

Mattes, R. and Bratton, M., 2003, 'Learning About Democracy in Africa, Performance and Experiences', Working Paper No. 29.

Melucci, A., 1996, 'Youth, Time and Social Movements', Available online at http:/www.alli.fi/nyri/young/1996artikkelMelucci2-96.htm

Nyamnjoh, F. and Nantang, B. J., 2002, 'African Universities in Crisis and the Promotion of a Democratic Culture: The Political Economy of Violence in African Educational Systems', *African Studies Review*, Vol.45, No. 2.

Olson, Mancur, 1971, [1965]. *The Logic of Collective Action : Public Goods and the Theory of Groups* (Revised edition ed.), Harvard University Press.

Osei-Hwedie, K., 1989, 'Youth Problem in a Changing World' in Osei-Hwedie K. and M. Ndulo eds., *Studies in Youth and Development, Commonwealth Youth Programme,* Multi-Media Publications, Lusaka.

The College Times, 2001, December Issue, No.3.

4. Eritrea

Post-war Politics and Higher Education Students in Eritrea

Berhane Berhe Araia

Introduction

Recent research projects have focused on students and youth in Africa. The situation of youth and students is the best barometer of a society's political and economic well being. The collapsing economies of African countries, neo-liberal and global ideologies, information technology and the image of the West are at the centre of discussions of structural constraints on youth and the agentic decisions young people make amid all the social problems. Africa, as a continent, has had diverse politico-economic experiences resulting in different challenges for young people.

Several African countries have plied a course of political developments from communal economy, autocratic governments to liberalized economy and electoral governance. In the 1980s and early 1990s, regime change occurred in several countries mainly as a result of pressure from civil society.[1] The pressures came not significantly in the form of deliberative and rational discussion that many theories advocate, but as a result of protests and demonstrations in major urban centers. Youth and students, in particular, figured prominently (as they have always been) in the history of post-colonial Africa. As Mahmood Mamdani put it,[2] the urban population rediscovered the discourse of 'rights' again for the second time since opposition to colonial governments. Since then, however, the situation of youth has not improved. It seems as if globalization is presenting youth and students with tastes that they cannot satisfy in their countries. Such a persistent problem has led some scholars to use the label 'lost generation'.[3] The marginalization of young people, at least in its present-day form, may be the overall structural consequence of the rise of neo-liberal capitalism.[4]

On the other hand, the role of African youth in the political arena is perceived as a significant departure from authoritarian enterprises inaugurated by the nationalist ruling classes. Mamadou Diouf[5] argues that the youth has played a crucial role in the configuration of nationalist coalitions and that they have been the first group in society to manifest, in practical and often violent ways, hostility toward the reconstituted nationalist movement. The manifestations of youth opposition may differ from country to country, as Lamont and Thevenot[6] acknowledge, because there are national cultural repertoires operating as cultural tools that are unevenly available across situation and national contexts. Along the same line, youth and students in Eritrea are challenging nationalist projects and the post-liberation discourses. Eritrea's political history and national cultural repertoire presents its youth with unique constraints and opportunities. Eritrea gained independence through a thirty-year armed struggle while many African countries were going through the transition to democratic forms of government. Eritrea's nation-building project was therefore a result of the long struggle for independence and has thus resulted in memories, experiences, perceptions and interpretations of events on the part of both the liberation movement leaders, on the one hand, and the receiving public on the other. Independent Eritrea's development and nation-building strategies are thus a mixture of these nationalist projects and commitments and the neo-liberal economic demands that the country's location brings.

After a bloody border war with Ethiopia, Eritrea's nationalist project has been challenged. University students played a prominent role in challenging national development projects and discourses. Comparatively speaking, the challenges and consequent political dissent and repression of student movements can be viewed in terms of the crisis of the single-party system in Africa.[7] Eritrea's experience is unique and, at the same time, similar to that of other African countries. It is similar in that students and youth have played an active role in relation to the state and its national projects as mediated through different institutions. It is unique for it still shows the power of nationalist duty-bound ideology, and contestations had to be more at the ideological or cultural level in order to be effective. In most African countries, mainly for reasons related to the historical period in question, contestations were for the most part framed materially, pregnant with such neoliberal consequences as rising inequality and economic deprivation, and corruption by state officials that aroused popular resentment. The salience of the nationalist ideology is manifested in issues of state legitimacy, citizen participation and war mobilization. Eritrea's pursuit of national autonomy through thirty years of war demonstrates the continuing importance of nationalism as an instrument for moulding and shaping collective identity and political aspirations.[8] It is therefore important to look at Eritrean students in higher education and analyze their perceptions and evaluations of their lives and involvement. It is important to investigate the role of nationalist ideology in students' life evaluations, their involvement in the political process and how their political demands are shaped and articulated.

Background: Discourses on Nationalism, Post-war Crisis and Student Opposition

Eritrea gained independence through a protracted thirty-year period of armed struggle and the requisite large-scale social mobilization. Independence came with its own collective memory, a euphoric nationalist feeling and a political culture that prioritized the national collective good over individual rights. Nationalist ideology, especially that of national duty, has dominated policy and political discourse in independent Eritrea. Eritrea is located in a region notorious for its history of inter-state conflicts and thus national defence has become central in determining national strategies and policies. The national development project had thus introduced a national service programme with multidimensional aims, including youth participation in development activities. National service for all adults aged 18 to 40 and a summer work programme for secondary school students were introduced in 1994. Both are mandatory for all young citizens of Eritrea. Students have been and still are actively involved in these national projects. Circumstances have, however, geared the national service programme more towards national defense rather than reconstruction and development.

Eritrea fought a border war with Ethiopia between 1998 and 2000 — a costly and devastating war by all standards. That war had a devastating effect, displacing a huge population and causing what appeared to be a long overdue split and dissent within the government and the ruling front[9] in 2001. Private newspapers started entertaining critical opinions and eventually the government banned all private newspapers in September 2001.[10] Dissenting government officials and newspaper editors have been in prison for over seven years, without any formal charges brought against them before a court of law. The government has collectively accused them of 'breach of national security'. In the same period, university students' opposition to part of the 2001 national summer work programme and the ensuing trials led to confrontations between the University Students' Union and the government, prompting the government to take harsh measures against the students.[11] Such unprecedented events could be considered the political opportunity seized by the youth to oppose state policy. Consequently, the president of the students' union was detained along with other students in a desert camp. The detention, which sadly resulted in the death of two students, was strongly condemned in both national and international circles.[12] Students opposed the national summer work programme for several reasons. The main reason raised in their negotiations with the university administration was their unmet demand for financial help to cover their educational expenses. Moreover, the students' union demanded autonomy in managing the summer projects and in its press statements questioned the legality of the summer programme, citing ILO labour conventions. Throughout the proceedings, the students' union presented itself both in newspaper articles and speeches as the protector not only of the interests of students but also of those of society at large.

Viewed from a political perspective, these events signal a crisis of legitimacy and a challenge to the nationalist discourse and practice that had enabled the government to introduce changes without much resistance from the population. In general, post-independence Eritrean history has been dominated by nationalist ideology — a powerful force that has lent legitimacy to the liberation front and ushered in macro-structural changes.[13] The political culture has been characterized by ambiguous nationalist discourse[14] and also by a culture that subordinated political creativity to the cult of efficiency and rationality.[15] Though there has not been any in-depth research on the political culture of Eritrea, its nationalist culture which gives priority to subordination and unity and, in particular, its discursive stress on unity of ideas has been regarded as a potential problem for the development of a vibrant public sector in Eritrea.[16] However, the aforementioned recent political events somehow mark a change from this nationalist political culture, notwithstanding the heavy-handedness of government's response to dissent and opposition.

Higher education institutions provide students with vital space for making far-reaching claims on citizenship issues in the national political system. The state and society also instill great expectations in students, especially higher education students, when it comes to nation-building and national development projects. The short-lived student movement at the University of Asmara touched on core issues relating to state legitimacy, the discourses and practices of citizenship and national identity in Eritrea. It questioned and challenged hitherto accepted discourses. Students were caught between making their case by dint of universalist arguments regarding national citizens' rights as well as particular issues pertaining to their participation in the immediate development projects.

These political events are worth investigating both for their relevance to the political history of Eritrea and its political generations, as well as for what the current reality in contemporary Eritrea represents in terms of comparative African history and politics. In terms of Eritrea's political history, national programmes that had gone unchallenged in theory and practice came under critical scrutiny by the student body. In such scrutiny, students referred to international human rights conventions, citizenship rights and their duty as educated citizens and to the socio-economic problems they face.[17] The university has also served as a forum for discussing several issues. The situation within the university was also discussed in the then private press.[18] There was a split between the government and the ruling front. Several fundamental political questions were raised by students and the government reacted by jailing the students' union president and forcibly moving the students into desert camps for the summer service. This highly politicized decision was condemned as a flagrant violation of basic human rights. No active student movement existed thereafter. However, one significant effect of this activism was the change in the nationalist pre-figurative political culture, described by some as a 'culture of silence'.[19] The student movement broke this culture of silence and questioned or disputed the received discourses and policy practices. However, its long-term effect is yet to be seen as student opposition to state practices is increasingly expressed in more individual, as opposed to, collective actions and decisions. .

From a comparative historical standpoint, Eritrea seems to be at the stage where most African countries were forty years ago, that is, shortly after they acquired independence. When most countries had had enough of autocratic power and were going for electoral democracies, Eritrea was still just emerging as an independent and sovereign country for the first time in its history. It was a time when many African economies were being liberalized and structural adjustment programmes were at the centre of national programmes. Around same period, large numbers of military and one-party dictatorships were crumbling in the face of massive civil protests and demands for political change.[20]

It is important to view students as a political generation,[21] and then study their perceptions of life situations, future aspirations and social involvement in the aftermath of such a contemporary chain of events. Two distinct political generations emerged from Eritrean political and popular discourse during the last war with Ethiopia: The '*Yeka'alo*' (the 'Can Do') and the '*Warsay*' (the 'Inheritor of the legacy'). The national service programme began on the premise that it would inculcate military discipline in post-war Eritrean youth and thus narrow the gap between the *tegadelti* (freedom fighters) and future generations,[22] the '*Warsays*', who were in their early teens when Eritrea was liberated. These terms were initially popularized by popular songwriters and subsequently became household words. The term '*Yeka'alo*' comes from a popular song of the late 1980s when the Eritrean People's Liberation Army destroyed the Ethiopian army in a strategic town in northern Eritrea. The term '*warsay*', which generally describes the national service generation, was popularized in 1998 after a famous song. In the same vein, the Eritrean government proposed a new rehabilitation programme in 2002 captioned the "*Warsay-Yeka'alo campaign*". In addition to discursive distinctions, this generational divide is manifest in political attitudes and power-sharing and possibly signals shifts in perception and levels of nationalism and citizenship.

Historical Evolution of Higher Education in Eritrea

The University of Asmara (UOA) is the only university in Eritrea. Although Eritrea had been an Italian colony since 1890, the development of higher education only dates back to the late 1950s when the University of Asmara was inaugurated. Unlike other colonial governments, the Italian colonial government limited native education to elementary level. The missionary congregation, Pie Madri della Nigrizia of Verona, Italy, officially established the UOA on 20 December 20 1958 when Eritrea was federated with Ethiopia by a United Nations resolution. It can be argued that the increase in the student population triggered the nationalist mobilization drive towards national liberation. In 1958, a famous demonstration was staged in Asmara when the Eritrean flag was replaced with that of Ethiopia and the two formal languages of the Eritrean government were replaced by the Ethiopian official language.[23] In that demonstration, the youth, especially students played a major role. Student mobilization and demonstrations were also instrumental in the revival of nationalist sentiments in 1960.[24] Thus, the same generation of students who flocked to universities in Eritrea and Ethiopia produced the leaders of the liberation movements and the ruling class of present-day Eritrea.

For the greater part of its history, the university was part of the Ethiopian higher education system and was relegated into specialized fields of study. It was only after the independence of Eritrea in 1991 that the university was restructured to meet the needs of the new nation. The restructuring enabled it to contribute to the nation-building process. In 1991, an international conference was organized to map out the principles and institutional structures for the reorganization of the university. Over the years, the university increased its fields of study and student population. The university had only 10 programmes in 1993 and these have grown to 45. The university of Asmara had about 5000 student in 2003. In Eritrea, education is free and the university offers free education, meals and dormitory facilities for those who come from outside Asmara. There are plans to introduce fees but such plans are still on paper. Fees do not even seem to be on the university's scale of priorities.

The future of higher education in Eritrea may follow trends similar to those in other African countries where the trend is to privatize universities and reduce state involvement in higher education. However, as of now, adjustment and liberalization in the educational sector have not affected higher education in Eritrea. Instead, the university's model and its relationship with the state and its students has taken a form of nation-building wherein educational expenses, including catering and dormitory expenses, are covered by the university and students are required to contribute to different national development projects through the national service programme.

Study Methods and Demographic Characteristics of Survey Respondents

This research was conducted as part of the CODESRIA comparative research network on Youth and Higher education. The data collection took place in the summer of 2003 in Asmara, Eritrea. The respondents were chosen using a purposive sampling method designed to make the sample representative of students from different fields of study, number of years in higher education and gender. It should be noted that the study was undertaken after the short-lived student movement and in a situation of post-war economic depression. It is therefore important to show how students view their life conditions and future life aspirations. The data collection methods used were a survey, in-depth interviews and archival research. Primarily, a questionnaire was developed, tested on thirty students, redesigned and finally administered to 96 students. The questionnaire consisted of 65 questions and the reporting in this paper is based on selected questions only. The analysis in this paper is based mainly on this survey data. Moreover, few selected interviews were conducted with students who were part of the students' union and others to further investigate students' perceptions and experiences. I also use archival data such as newspaper articles, speeches and communiqués to relate some important events.

Table 1 describes the characteristics of survey respondents. The sample is 72 per cent male and 28 per cent female. This is representative of the student population at the University of Asmara, for example, in 1998. Students who joined the university were 86 per cent male and 14 per cent female and for 2002, the student population was 90 per cent male and 10 per cent female. These two batches would correspond to fourth-year and first-year students in this sample. The sample also consists of students from different faculties: Social Sciences (32.3), Education (12.5), Law (10.4), Natural Science (12.5), Business (8.3), Health Sciences (13.5), Agriculture and Engineering (10.4). Eighty-three per cent of the students have participated at least in one summer work programme whereas 57 per cent of them have completed military training as part of their national obligation.

Table 1: Descriptive Statistics of Demographic Characteristics of Respondents (N= 96)

	Percentage
Male	72
Female	28
First Year	7.3
Second Year	18.8
Third year	38.5
Fourth Year	26
Fifth Year	9.4
Have been in summer work programmes	83
Have been employed	33
Have completed military service	57.3

Background Characteristics and School Performance

Family background is one of the most important factors that affect students' performance, social involvement and future life plans. One way of looking at the role of family background in student academic performance is to see how family responsibilities interfered with schoolwork among students. Family responsibility is important as it indicates social living arrangements of students and it would potentially influence students' perceptions and actions in other domains of their lives. In the University of Asmara, only students coming from outside the city of Asmara are allowed to stay on campus. A question was included in the survey that asked students whether family responsibilities interfered with the student's schoolwork. Results are presented in Table 2 showing the frequency of interference in relation to the residence status of students.

An overall mean test difference shows statistically significant difference in the mean of interference frequency reported (Chi-Square is 8.9, p= .038) among those who live on campus, with relatives, with parents and by themselves. A look at the mean frequencies of each of these categories shows that, students living with relatives report the highest frequency of family responsibility interfering with their schoolwork. This may be due to the nature of the relationship, as living with relatives puts more pressure on students to help with family matters. The groups with the second highest reported frequency of family interferences are those who live on campus and this may have to do with the obligation they feel because they are unable to help their families in the day-to-day activities. Those who stay with parents or by themselves are less likely to report interference of family responsibilities in their schoolwork. They have on average a mean value that is less than the total mean value. In sum, students living at home, whether with parents or by themselves are at an advantage of not having family responsibility interfering with their academic work.

However, there is no significant difference with respect to gender of the students in the level of family responsibility interference. This is interesting in light of the low level of female enrolment in tertiary education and the explanation usually given is that female students bear a lot of responsibilities at home. But this may be due to self-selection of the female students, as once they have joined the university, they are less likely to take on more family responsibility that they otherwise would. With respect to the religion of the family in which the students were raised, there is no significant difference in the reporting of family interference from students coming from different religious backgrounds.

Table 2: Since entering the university, indicate, "How often you felt that your family responsibilities interfered with your schoolwork?"

Residence	Mean	Gender	Mean	Religion	Mean
Total	2.75*	Total	2.75**	Total	2.73***
Stay on campus	2.96	Male	2.74	None	3.0
Stay with relatives	3.17	Female	2.78	Orthodox	2.65
Stay with parents	2.42			Catholic	3.0
Stay alone by yourself	2.5			Protestant	2.25
				Moslem	2.80

Note: N=96, (1 not at all, 2= rarely, 3= occasionally, 4=frequently).
*Chi-Sq=8.9, DF= 4, p=.038, ** Chi-Sq= .035, DF=1, P=.85, ***Chi-Sq= 3.2, DF=2, p=.49

One way of evaluating students' experiences in higher education is to study their evaluations of the benefits they get from institutions of higher learning. The way students evaluate their university experiences is based on their background characteristics such as family residences, gender and military service experiences and these in turn determine students' evaluations of their future life plans and aspirations. Students were asked how much their knowledge in different fields and areas, understanding of several issues and their involvement in student matters changed during their stay at the university. Statistical results are reported in Table 3. Overall, more improvements in knowledge of fields of study is reported followed by critical thinking, general knowledge and global issues respectively by all students. Students report the lowest average of improvement in their knowledge of people from different cultures. Breaking down results by students of different residences, we find significant differences only in the knowledge of people from different cultures and understanding of global issues. Students who live on campus report the highest improvement in their knowledge of people from different cultures as a result of their stay in the university. This clearly would be due to the opportunities for interaction which the university living arrangements provided to students. On the other hand, students who live with their parents report better understanding of global issues as a result of their stay in the university.

There is almost no significant difference between male and female students in the amount of reported changes in knowledge in different areas. Overall, students report that their knowledge and understanding has remained about the same or increased during their stay at the university. Previous military service experience, however, produces some significant differences in certain areas of knowledge and involvement. Students who have not done any military service by far report that they have acquired better knowledge in their fields of study whereas students who have done military service are more likely to report that they have gained a greater understanding of social problems facing the country during their stay in the university. As a result, students with military service experience are more likely to report that their ability to think critically and their involvement in issues that affect students have increased as well. Therefore, prior military service coupled with better knowledge of social problems results in more student involvement.

Current Life Perception and Future Life Plans

One's life plan is articulated within the overarching cultural norms and historical values of a given society. Thus, individuals plot the trajectory of their lives on the societal map, based on actual and perceived uncertainties surrounding current structural conditions. The perception of African youth and the level of agency they occupy paradoxically have been perceived as constrained and creative. The collapsing economies and failing political systems have led to the view that African youth are "a lost generation".[25] In this light, youths are perceived as *powerless*, exploited and homogenous in their experiences. In another perspective, they are simultaneously the "terrors of the present" or "errors of the past" and in some cases, "the prospect of a future".[26] Following the former view, students often tend to portray themselves as demoralized individuals who are unlikely to see themselves as bearers of civil and political powers with the identity and status of full citizenship. On the other hand, the status of students has a liberalizing effect granting that the absence of parental control gives students a chance to undertake various social experimentations with their personal and social identities. Thus, students in higher education occupy an important societal position in terms of individual social mobility and involvement in social and political issues of consequence to society at large. In this section, we look at students' future life aspirations and plans and how they perceive their future and the future of the country in light of their experiences and socio-economic background.

In contemporary Eritrea, the post-war crisis and the prolonged military mobilization of youth for war efforts has disrupted the life plans of many young men and women. In relative terms, university students are more privileged and have more predictable life trajectories than their counterparts in the national service. However, given the country's economic and political situation students may not feel that their lives are so predictable in the long term. Many students have also participated both in military service and summer work programmes. As aforementioned, students have demonstrated a certain level of opposition to national service projects that led to brutal confrontation with state authorities. It is therefore the central part of this study to find out the differences in life aspirations and plans among those who have had experiences in these programmes and those who did not have. A central assumption here is that military mobilization might have resulted in altering the trajectory of the life course of many students and their perception and future prospects. In general, military service is a major disruptive factor in the life course, although the effects of service in a peacetime army are less deleterious. States intervene most drastically in the lives of their citizens when they are at war.[27]. The best way to capture such changes is in the perception of current life position and future life plans of students. Several factors affect students' perception of their situation and prospects. Thus we will also look at the impact of students' family residences, gender and religiosity on their life plans and perceptions.

The survey included a question on how predictable students think their current life situation is, on a scale from 'not at all predictable' to 'very predictable'. Overall, students on average think that their lives are between 'somewhat unpredictable' to 'pretty predictable'. The results from ANOVA mean differences show a significant difference in the mean value of predictability (F-value= 2.92, p= .025) among those who live on campus, with relatives, with parents and by themselves. The result shows that relatively those who live with parents score higher on predictability followed by those who live by themselves and with parents and those who live on campus score the lowest. This residence variable indicates much more than residence. The university's policy is such that only people who come from outside the city of Asmara are allowed to stay on campus. So those

Table 3: Since entering the university, "How have the following things changed?"

	Male	Female	Total
Your general knowledge	4.1	4.0	4.07
Your knowledge of your field	4.34	4.3	4.33
Your knowledge of people from different cultures	3.66	3.74	3.68
Your understanding of social problems facing our nation	3.81	3.7	3.78
Your understanding of global issues	3.97	4.0	3.99
Your ability to think critically	4.26	4.33	4.28
Your involvement in issues that affect students	3.4	3.5	3.44
Completed military service	**No**	**Yes**	**Total**
Your general knowledge	4.16	3.95	4.07
Your knowledge of your field	4.07	4.53	4.33**
Your knowledge of people from different cultures	3.73	3.61	3.68
Your understanding of social problems facing our nation	3.91	3.61	3.78*
Your understanding of global issues	4.05	3.9	3.99
Your ability to think critically	4.38	4.17	4.29*
Your involvement in issues that affect students	3.62	3.18	3.43**
Residence (Stay on campus, with relatives, with parents, alone by yourself) Total			
Your general knowledge			4.07
Your knowledge of your field			4.33
Your knowledge of people from different cultures			3.68*
Your understanding of social problems facing our nation			3.78
Your understanding of global issues			3.99*
Your ability to think critically			4.29
Your involvement in issues that affect students			3.43

Notes: (1= much worse, 2= worse, 3= about the same, 4= better, 5= much better)

** $P<.05$, * $p<0.1$

who stay on campus are those who come from outside the city and would be more likely to come from less privileged families. Besides, the support the other students get from parents and relatives may have increased the sense of predictability of lives among the other groups. As to those who live by themselves, it may have to do with self-selection with those better endowed with resources living by themselves and thus having better scores.

With respect to gender, there is a significant difference in the ways male and female students perceive the predictability of their future. Female students are more likely to report that their current life situation is predictable. This is an important finding in the context of future life plans of both sexes. For example, female students are more likely to report that they will get married in the next ten years than are male students.[28] Thus, female students may feel they have more life opportunities and that may be the reason for their reporting a more predictable current life situation. Interestingly, students who have been to military service training are not in any statistically significant way less likely to report that their lives are unpredictable. However, students who have never been to any summer work programme are slightly more likely to report that their current live situation is predictable. One's religiosity is important in giving meaning to life thereby making people feel that their lives are predictable. Religious commitment has also offered many young people a way of escape from social marginalization.[29] However, the mean difference test results do not show any significant differences among students who attach varying levels of importance of religion in their lives. That is, students' levels of religiosity do not affect their perceptions of the predictability of their current life situation.

A related variable that indicates students' current reality and future life plan is whether students live their lives without much thought for the future. On average, students disagreed with the statement that 'they live without much thought for the future', indicating that they think a lot about the future. Similarly, there was a statistically significant difference in the level of agreement to the statement "You live your life without much thought for the future" (Chi-Square17.4, p= .027) among those who live on campus, with relatives, with parents and by themselves. In the same pattern as in the case of life predictability, those living on campus tend to report less disagreement with the statement that they live their lives without much thought for the future. With respect to gender, male and female students equally disagree with the statement that they are living their lives without much thought for the future. In other words, there is no significant difference among them. Both report that they are living with much thought for their future. In like manner, there is no difference between those who have completed their military service and those who did not in their disagreement with the proposition that living without much thought for the future. All report that they are not living without thought of the future.

University students are relatively privileged in general. Moreover, in the context of Eritrea, as many youth are serving in the national defence forces even including former university graduates, it is safe to argue that university students occupy the most privileged social position. Fifty seven per cent of the respondents have also gone through military training at one point in time. Therefore, it is logical to expect that students will develop evaluations of their life situations in comparison with people of the same age who are not able to study at the university. Thus, the respondents were asked: i:'Compared to other people of your age outside the university, how successful are you?' on a scale from 'very successful' to 'not at all successful'. On the average, student responses fall between 'slightly' and 'not at all' successful. That is, university students do not think that they are more successful than their age counterparts who do not study in higher education. A mean difference analysis shows (Tables 4 and 5) that there are no significant differences in how successful students think of themselves compared to their peers outside the university along residence, gender and military service status of students. Overall, students report that they are between 'slightly successful' and 'not at all successful' compared to other people of the same age outside the university.

Career Choice and Life Plans

It is important at this point to consider the career choices students have and the importance they attach to different career choices. Students' preferences for their future careers reflect both their conceptions of success and their perceptions of reality of the country and the times they live in. The investigation of future career plans is important not simply because it may enable us to determine the degree to which student career aspirations are met, but more importantly because such information reveals the values which are likely to guide students behavior.[30] To explore the dimension of career choice, respondents were asked what their plans are after graduation. Respondents were also asked to consider the importance of future career choices in five areas: I). To get further education, II) A career in the private business sector, III) A career in government, IV) A career in the NGO sector and V) Becoming successful in a business of your own. Respondents rated the importance of each of these career choices on a scale that ranges from 'not important' to 'essential'.

The first results presented are about what actual plans students have after graduation. Thirty six per cent of the students plan to get a job after graduation whereas thirty-four per cent of them plan to leave the country for further studies. A chi-square difference test between plan of future career in NGO and the different plans do not demonstrate any significant dependence between them (Chi-Sq= 15.4, p=. 64) whereas the same test (Chi-Sq= 56.4, p=. 000) shows a relationship between the importance of getting further education and these different plans. This can be interpreted in a way, as those who think getting higher education

Table 4: "How Predictable is your Current Life Situation?"

Residence	Mean Value	Gender	Mean Mean	Military service	Mean value	Summer student service	Mean value	Religiosity	value value
Total	2.43*	Total	2.44 **	Total	2.43***	Total	2.43+	Total	2.44++
Stay on campus service	2.2	Male	2.31	Military service	2.35	Summer	2.37	Essential	2.48
Stay with relatives	2.3	Female	2.74	No military	2.54	No summer	2.75	Very important	2.52
Stay with parents	2.7							Somewhat important	2.1
Stay alone by yourself	2.5							Not important	2.5

Note: (1= not at all predictable, 2= somewhat unpredictable, pretty predictable, 4= very predictable).
*Chi-Sq=7.5, DF=4, p=.025, *Chi-Sq=3.5, DF=1, p=.024, ***Chi-Sq=.79, DF=1, P=.29,

+Chi-Sq=1.95, DF=1, p=.09, ++ Chi-Sq=3.5, DF=4, P=.29

Table 5: Thought for future and perception of success

Residence	Thought for the future	How successful	Gender	Thought for the future	How successful	Military service	Thought for the future	How successful
	Mean value	Mean value		Mean value	Mean value		Mean value	Mean value
Total	1.67*	3.36+	Total	1.67**	3.36++	Total	1.67***	1.67***
Stay on campus	2.07	3.15	Male	1.66	3.34	Military service	1.6	3.3
Stay with relatives	1.2	3.5	Female	1.66	3.34	No military service	1.76	3.6+++
Stay with parents	1.29	3.55						
Stay alone by yourself	1.0	3.5						

Notes: N=94, "you live your life without much thought for the future "(1= strongly disagree, 2= slightly disagree, 3= neither agree nor disagree, 4= slightly agree, 5= strongly agree).

N=95, "Compared to other people of your age outside the university, how successful are you?" (1= very successful, 2= moderately successful, 3= slightly successful, 4= not at all successful)

*Chi-Sq=17.4, DF=4, p=. 027, **Chi-Sq=. 042, DF=1, p=. 87, ***Chi-Sq=. 54, DF=1, P=. 57,

+Chi-Sq=4, DF=1, p=. 13, ++Chi-Sq=. 079, DF=1, p=. 71, +++Chi-Sq=. 31, DF=1, P=. 46

is more important for their future are more likely to report wanting to have postgraduate training and leaving the country for further education as well. So in general, getting higher education seems to be the most important way to get mobility for the future for most students in Eritrea.

The results demonstrate that leaving the country to work elsewhere accounts for only 6.3 per cent of students. These results are in stark contrast to the survey on Zimbabwean students. Among the Zimbabwean students, leaving the country to work elsewhere is the plan for 31 per cent of students whereas leaving the country for further studies accounts for only 9 per cent of student plans. This, in part, can be explained by the big number of postgraduate students studying in South Africa under the Eritrean government's human resources development programme and the fact that further education remains as the only way for young people to leave Eritrea. That is to say, the Eritrean students see leaving the country for further education as a way of social mobility whereas for Zimbabwean students employment migration is the best hope.

Table 6: What are your Plans after you finish your Training/Degree? (Comparison of Eritrean and Zimbabwean Students)

	Eritrea Sample (N=96)	Zimbabwe Sample (N=96)
Get a Job	36.5%	47.9%
Pursue higher degree (post graduate)	18.8%	9.4%
Leave country for further studies	34.4%	9.4%
Leave country to work elsewhere	6.3%	31.3
Other	4.1%	—

Upon considering occupations students desired, the striking finding is the similarity of responses between both genders as well as between those of different military training status. Overall, a career in the NGO sector is the most important choice for many students while a career in government is ranked of lowest importance in their future career plans. Becoming successful in one's own business is the second most valued career choice for all students in the sample. Planning to get further education has a mean value of importance that puts it third out of the five choices provided to students. However, a career in the private sector is ranked as the second lowest important career choice for students. This pattern is almost the same for both genders and students with different military service completion status. All career choices, but for the NGO sector, have the same mean value of importance for both male and female students. More female than male students reported that a career in the NGO sector is so important to their future career plan. Though not statistically significant, the mean value of importance of becoming successful in one's own business is higher for males while that of government career is higher for female students.

Table 7: Importance of Future Goals: Means on Selected Variables, by Gender, and by Military Service Status

Comparison of Male and Female Students		
	Male	Female
1. To get further education	3.94	3.96
2. A career in the private business sector	3.63	3.59
3. A career in government	2.59	2.73
4. A career in the NGO sector	4.37*	4.85*
5. Becoming successful in a business of your own	4.34	4.04
Comparison of those who completed military service with those who didn't		
1. To get further education	3.94	3.95
2. A career in the private business sector	3.55	3.71
3. A career in government	2.61	2.63
4. A career in the NGO sector	4.50	4.51
5. Becoming successful in a business of your own	4.26	4.24

Notes: All items scored 1 (not important) to 5 (Essential). *P<. 01

Student Involvement

Student involvement in politics takes place in two interrelated arenas - the university campus and the world beyond its gates.[31] As indicated in the previous section, one of the reasons for the summer 2001 student union confrontation with the government was the involvement of students in matters that affect them and their ever-growing demands for involvement in the planning of the national summer work programme for that year. The issues raised were primarily related to terms of payments of the summer programme but the different communiqués issued by the student's union at that time show that students were raising wide-ranging questions. Many people outside the university criticized the students' demand for payment as being self-interested, especially as many youth were still serving in the mobilized national defence forces without pay. Thus, students' communiqués argued strongly that they were doing this for the national good and tried to defend themselves against arguments of self-interest.[32]

Older research on African students suggests that the 'politics of self-interest' enables students to challenge the state when their interests are directly threatened and support it when it suits them.[33]

Relying on student surveys on Ghana, Tanzania and Uganda, Barkan argues that politically active students in the industrial world focus their attention on problems that have little to do with their material self-interest whereas students in his sample were mainly driven by self-interest. Thus, he concludes that entry of African students into the political arena is motivated less by idealistic and ideological concerns and more by concern for personal gain. These observations made in a study done in the early 1970s correspond to the immediate post-independence period of those countries and we use those conclusions as starting questions to investigate what determines student involvement in political issues among University of Asmara students. We ask whether it is self-interest or knowledge or the perception of their position in society that determines students' involvement.

In this study, rather than making a distinction between in-campus and outside involvement, the question probed respondents' levels of involvement that affect them both on campus and elsewhere during their stay in the university. Respondents were asked to rate their involvement on a Likert scale, i.e. whether it has decreased, remained about the same or increased over the time they have been at the university.

The results (Table 8) from the involvement question show that there is no difference among male and female students and the number of years in the university and the field of study of students on levels of involvement in issues that affect students. However, completion of military service results show a significant difference in student involvement. Those who completed military service have an average of 3.62 while those who never did any military service have a 3.18 mean score of involvement. On the other hand, those who completed one or more summer work programmes is not different in terms of involvement from those who have never done any summer work programme. This may be a result of the experiences military training provided students, thus leading them to be more involved in changing their situation.

Table 8: ANOVA Table of Mean Differences in Involvement that Affects Students

	F-value	P-value
Comparison of male and female students .	35	.55
Comparison of students of different years of study	.89	0.47
Comparison of students who stay on campus and with parents	1.38	.24
Comparison of students from different faculties	.45	.86
Comparison between those who completed military service and those who didn't	6.74	.01*
Comparison between those who have been to summer work and those who didn't	.23	.62

Notes: Involvement was measured with the question "Since entering the university, how much has been your involvement in issues that affect students", and codes 1(much worse) to 5(much better). *P< .05 level of significance.

A further look at results from correlation of involvement with selected variables shows that there is a modest significant relationship between those who think they will get a well paying job after graduation and their involvement in issues that affect students. Students who think that they are less likely to get a well-paying job also report less involvement. On the other hand, students' age and the number of times one has been in summer work programmes do not have any significant correlation with student involvement, though signs indicate that with age involvement decreases while with the increase in the number of summer work programmes students' level of involvement increases. There is a positive relationship between students benefiting from different activities in their stay in the university with their involvement. That is, the greater the reported change in understanding of social problems facing the country, the greater the knowledge of people from different cultures, the more improvement in student involvement reported. Similarly, improvement in ability to think critically and in understanding of global issues and knowledge of one's field of study have a mild positive correlation that is, the students who reported an increase in those areas of knowledge and understanding are also more likely to report that their individual involvement also increased. In sum, these correlations indicate that involvement is more influenced by changes in one's perception of local and global issues and less by perception of one's prospects for future success. In a way, this supports the view of the university as a space that provides students with ideas for activism and involvement.

Table 9: Correlation of Student Involvement with Selected Variables

	Correlation coefficient t
Will get a well-paying job after graduation +	-.32**
Age	-.14
Number of summer work programmes involved	.056
Understanding of social problems facing our nation	.41**
Knowledge of people from different cultures	.43**
Ability to think critically	.33**
Understanding of global issues	.21*
Knowledge of your field	.21*

Note: ** Correlation is significant at the 0.01 level (2-tailed),
* Correlation is significant at the 0.05 level (2-tailed).
+ 1= almost certain, 2= a good chance, 3= a 50-50 chance, 4= some chance, 5= no chance

However, correlations analysis does not give a definitive answer to the issue of causal direction. Thus, I estimate OLS regression models (Table 10) of student involvement as a function of the same variables. Model 1 includes whether students think they will get a well-paying job after graduation as a predictor. The responses for the prospective job variable were coded from 1 (almost certain) to 5 (no chance). Results show a significant negative effect of future job prospect variable on level of involvement. This is interpreted as follows: the lower students perceive their prospects of getting well-paying jobs, the lower the levels of involvement in student matters they also report. Thus, students who perceive the prospect of a well-paying job after graduation are also more likely to get involved in student matters during their stay in the university.

The addition of age and number of summer work programmes students attended do not improve the overall regression model and are not significant predictors of involvement. However, the addition of a series of variables that tap into students' intellectual experiences at the university improves the model. But only those who report to have gained a greater understanding of social problems facing Eritrea are more likely to report that they have increased their level of involvement in issues that affect students in general. Changes in other areas of knowledge such as global issues, field of study and critical thinking do not in any statistically significant way determine student involvement. Interestingly, however, the perception of future prospective jobs consistently in all models reduces the level of students' involvement. Thus, students who don't think they will get a well-paying job are less likely to report increased involvement as a result of their stay in the university. However, the magnitude of the effect of future job perception is less than that of the reported change in understanding of national problems and it is therefore safe to say that on average students' involvement and participation is determined more by knowledge and perception of national issues, followed by personal prospect of career and employment. This interpretation is supported both by the arguments that conceptualize the university as a sphere that teaches students to be more cognizant of social issues and it also speaks to the nationalist discourse of duty and obligation that is prevalent in Eritrea. This is not to say that self-interest and perception of future prospects of individual students do not matter. Rather, as the results show, self-interested perceptions do determine students' involvement but that students' involvement is more likely to be determined by the changes in students' knowledge and understanding.

Table 10: Regression of Student Involvement on Selected Variables

	Model 1	Model 2	Model 3
Will get a well-paying job after graduation	-.27 (.08)*	-.26 (.08)*	-.192 (.087)*
Age		-.017 (.02)	-.023 ((.021)
Number of summer work programmes involved		.05 (.07)	.062 (.067)
Understanding of social problems facing our nation			301 (.117)*
Ability to think critically			.097 (.178)
Understanding of global issues			.051 (.136)
Knowledge of your field			.068 (.105)
R-Square	.104	.12	.26
R	.32	.35	.51

Notes: Results in parentheses are standard error values.
          * Indicates level of significance at the .05 level.

Discussion

Our investigation of the students at the University of Asmara was more of an exploratory research and thus looked at many aspects of the students' lives. It investigated the students' educational experiences, their current life situation and future career plans as well as their involvement in maters that affect students' lives. The analysis of the data collected on the students reveals interesting patterns. The study suggests that residence at home puts students at an advantage of having to focus on their academic work without much interference of family responsibilities. Interestingly, female students are not more likely than male students to be disadvantaged by family responsibilities. On the other hand, campus living enables students to get acquainted with people of different cultural background and thus socializes them well. Both male and female students report that they have gotten more knowledge in their respective fields of study and their ability to think critically has increased as a result of their university education.

The analysis demonstrates that students do not think their current life situations are predictable. On average, students think that their life is between 'somewhat unpredictable' to 'pretty predictable'. These results are expected, given the current conditions prevailing in the country. However, family support mediates the feeling of life predictability and thus those who can count on family support are more likely to feel that their current life is more predictable. In addition, female students felt a greater sense of predictability, perhaps partly because the national service puts more pressure on male students. Another interesting finding from the study is that, irrespective of the experience of military service and the level of religiosity students feel, all students think that their life is between 'somewhat unpredictable' to 'pretty predictable'. The results are somewhat surprising as they suggest that students' prior national service experience as well as being so religiously involved does not in any significant way determine whether their life is predictable or not.

Along the same line, all students irrespective of gender, military service status, or residence status do not think they are living their lives without thinking much of the future. That is, students do a lot of thinking about their future lives and they are concerned and have future career and other life plans. Certainly, this shows students are not a 'lost generation' without much of future plans but instead think a lot about the future. Individuals make evaluations of their lives in comparison to people in their countries with similar characteristics. The analysis shows that overall university students do not think they are more successful in their lives than other youth of the same age who are not in the university. Students feel only slightly successful if any. This is an interesting finding compared to the relative advantage university students have. As will be discussed shortly, their involvement is more influenced by their evaluation of their life chances as not significantly different from others of the same age.

In terms of social mobility and career choice of students, getting a job and leaving the country for further education are the most perceived ways of social mobility and success among Asmara university students. In terms of job desirability and level of importance, NGO sector jobs are the most desirable jobs followed by self-owned business. On the other hand, government jobs are the least desirable jobs. These results reflect the economic rewards for the respective jobs in light of the fact that university graduates in the civil service are still working under the national service programme only for pocket money.

Results have shown that both material perception and idealistic concerns and perception are significant predictors of students' involvement. Unlike Barkan's assertion, however, students in Eritrea are more likely to think their involvement as coming from bigger concerns for national issues than material self-interest. Moreover, involvement levels do not significantly differ in terms of social experiences such as age and service experience but are significantly determined by future career prospects and perceived improvement in understanding of the national problem during their stay at university. As previously discussed, the student movement of summer 2001 tried hard in its discourses to claim its questions were not driven by self-interest of students but more for concern for university autonomy and the role of university students in the society. It placed importance on the obligation higher education provides students to question authority and national projects. The argument seems elitist in the sense of claiming students' role in the public sphere. Similarly, Mamdani (1995), discussing the role of the university in African societies, argues that the question of academic freedom and university autonomy began to take a political meaning for students and academics against state authoritarianism and growing fiscal crisis. He further argues that even as students battled, often inspired by larger social concerns, or the demand for university autonomy, they remained unshaken by elitist assumptions that they are true representatives of the populations. Such elitist tones, however, exist in students' perception of their life situation as they do in the perception of other youth in the country at large. Thus, students' political involvement in national projects and discourse also takes into account the reality that students share with other Eritrean youth in the political and economic situation of the country.

Conclusion

In conclusion, the case study shows that the Eritrean higher education system provides students with the knowledge and space for activism and that students' involvement is more influenced by their awareness of the social problems of the country and perception of their social position and responsibilities than by their material well-being and future prospects. The research has also shown that Eritrean higher education students feel a low level of predictability of their lives though they are far from a 'lost generation' who do not give much thought to the future.

Rather, they hold seemingly elitist discourses on their role in challenging national projects and policies, but this perception is compounded by the assessment of students' positions as being significantly better than that of other youth in Eritrea. Thus, it seems that they feel they represent and speak on behalf of other youth in Eritrea. Overall, student activism and involvement in higher education are driven both by self-interest and nationalist perception of their social roles in society.

The future of higher education in Eritrea and the role of the University of Asmara remains uncertain as the university has not admitted any new students for the last three years as there is a policy shift to start new technical colleges at the expense of the university. Even though the research findings from this paper cannot confidently make any predictions on the future of higher education and student activism in Eritrea, recent developments clearly have thwarted the developments gained as a result of the short-lived student activism of 2001. The prospects for democratic transition are receding in Eritrea and there is no space for open political activism. Only time will tell what forms of engagement student activism will take in the near future.

Notes

1. Bratton and Van de walle, 1997.
2. Mamdani, 1998
3. e.g. O'Brien, 1996.
4. Camaroff and Camaroff, 2001.
5. Diouf, 1996
6. Lamont and Thevenot, 2001.
7. Mamdani, 1994.
8. Calhoun, 1997: 122.
9. The publishing of a letter by some Eritrean academics abroad, and later, on the open letter distributed by some senior members of the Ruling Front and member of the National Assembly have changed the political scene. This was an event that senior members of the Eritrean ruling party, the People's Front for Democracy and Justice (PFDJ) have, for the first time ever, openly criticized President Issayas Afewerki. (UN Integrated Regional Information Networks, June 5, 2001).
10. An Eritrean National Assembly session held in January 2002 addressed the issue of the private press and set up a commission to establish a 'responsible' independent press. The Eritrean government has stressed that the ban on the private press is a 'temporary suspension' and that its commitment to the growth of a free press is on track. In the same session, the draft laws for election and formation of political parties were repealed, and the former was ratified while the law for the formation of political parties is postponed since 'the majority of the population required that it is not timely for political parties to be established.' To date, no private press exists in Eritrea.
11. The birth of the students' union in the university dates back to 1998, when the university administration took the initiative to form the union. Once the union was established, it played an important role in mobilizing students during the three rounds of

offensives from Ethiopia. It organized the mobilization of students for military training, donation of blood from students and other important activities. In the summer of 2001, unlike its previous activities, it started becoming more assertive in campaigning for students' rights.

12. On 22 August, it was reported that university teachers were convening a meeting on the condition of the students starting on 20 August. On 26 August, a local NGO, Citizens for Peace, condemned the measure taken against the student by the government and called for the release of the university student. Source: Keste Debena Newspaper, 22 August 2001. On the other hand, the HRW in a report titled *Escalating Crackdown in Eritrea, Reformists, Journalists, Students at Risk*, New York, September 21 2001, (also available online at www.Hrw.org) discusses how students at the University of Asmara, the only one in the country, had joined in criticizing the government by demanding better treatment from the government and consultation on matters that concern them.
13. Tronvoll, 1998
14. Iyob, 1997
15. Makki, 1996
16. For example, Calhoun, 1995.
17. In a graduation ceremony speech the students' union president spoke on the issue of contention between students and the university about the 'summer work programme'. He argued that the main factors for the opposition include legal, administrative and economic considerations. Under the administrative problems, he talked about the university being an autonomous institution. 'The university should not receive instructions from any government body. Giving autonomy to a university demonstrates readiness to work for the advancement of your subjects.' In terms of the legal aspect of the matter, he posed a question: 'Is this programme justified under the law? Eritrea is a signatory to the international conventions of ILO. The role of university students, in general, and the students' union in particular can be tremendous in this context. If we can give students full responsibility to handle the summer work programme by themselves, there is no reason why we should not expect an efficient implementation of it.
18. Many editors and journalists in the private newspapers were gradates of the University of Asmara or registered students who have had the same experiences was the students of the university.
19. Iyob, 1997
20. Bangura, 2000
21. In addition to sharing similar developments and historical experiences, they can be considered as a political generation, since they have become aware of their historical position and came together to try to work for social and political change (Braungart and Braungart 1986).
22. Iyob, 1997.
23. The federal arrangement stipulated that Eritrea would have its own flag, which it received from the UN, and that Tigrinya and Arabic will be the official languages. This was put in the Eritrean Constitution drafted by a UN representative, Anzo Matienzo.
24. Ammar, 1997.
25. Ammar, 1997.

26. Comaroff and Comaroff, 2001, pp. 33
27. Mayer and Schoepflin, 1990.
28. A mean differences test between male and female students on the probability of their being married in ten years time (Chi-Sq = 14.5, p =. 005). Female students were more certain that they will get married in the coming ten years while on average, male students thought there was 50 per cent chance of that happening.
29. O'Brien, 1996.
30. Barkan, 1975, p. 54.
31. Thousands of students and other youth have left Eritrea since the original writing of this chapter in 2004. The further totalitarization of the Eritrean state and lack of hope for future improvements in the political and economic situation of the country has forced thousands to leave the national army and national service projects and seek refuge in neighboring countries and furthermore into Europe and the Americas.
32. In the same graduation speech, the students' union president after saying that: '*University students have demonstrated their devotion to the motherland in the war against the Woyane*,' he goes on to say that a nation or government does not need support at wartime only. 'If we are to understand the concept of "support" only in the context of war, then we can confidently declare the nation is not getting the right support from its university students. We should also expect them to carry out in-depth studies and evaluations of policies and procedures drawn up and implemented by the Government as well as engage in the promotion of the rule of law.
33. Barkan, 1975, p. 129

References

Ammar, W-Y., 1997, 'The role of Asmara Students in the Eritrean Nationalist Movements: 1958-1968', *Eritrean Studies Review*, Vol.12, No. 1.

Bangura, Y., 2000, 'Democratization, Equity and Stability: African Politics and Societies in the 1990s', in Dharam Ghai ed., *Renewing Social and Economic Progress in Africa*, .New York: St. Martin's Press, Inc.

Barkan, J., 1975, *An African Dilemma: University Students, Development and Politics in Ghana, Tanzania and Uganda*, Nairobi: Oxford University Press.

Bratton, M. and Nicolas van de W., 1997, *Democratic Experiments in Africa: Regime transitions in Comparative Perspective*, Cambridge, U.K.; New York: Cambridge University Press.

Braungart, R. G. and Margaret, M. B., 1986, 'Life-Course and Generational Politics', *Annual Review of Sociology*, Vol. 12. pp. 205-231.

Calhoun, C., 1995, 'Civil Society, Nation-Building and Democracy: The Importance of the Public Sphere to the Constitutional Process', a paper presented at the International Symposium on the making of the Eritrean Constitution.

Calhoun, C., 1997, *Nationalism*, Minneapolis: University of Minnesota Press.

Diouf, M., 1996, 'Urban Youth and Senegalese Politics: Dakar 1988-1994', *Public Culture*, Vol. 8, pp. 225-250.

Iyob, R., 1997, 'The Eritrea Experiment: A Cautious Pragmatism?' *Journal of Modern African Studies*, Vol. 35 No. 4, pp.647-673.

Lamont and Thevenot, 2001, *Rethinking Comparative Cultural Sociology: Repertoires of Evaluation in France and the United States*, Cambridge University Press.

Makki, F., 1996, 'Nationalism, State Formation and the Public Sphere: Eritrea' *Review of African Political Economy,* Vol. 23, No. 70..

Mamdani, M., 1998, 'The Politics of Civil Society and Ethnicity: Reflections on an African Dilemma', in Diane Davis, ed., *Political Power and Social Theory*, Vol. 12.

Mamdani, M., 1994, 'Introduction', in M. Mamdani and M. Diouf., eds., *Academic Freedom,* Dakar: CODESRIA.

Mayer, K.U., and Urs, S., 1989, 'The State and the Life Course', *Annual Review of Sociology*, Vol. 15, pp. 187-209.

O'Brien, D. C., 1996,– 'A Lost Generation? Youth Identity and State Decay in West Africa', in Richard Werbner and Terence Ranger eds., *Post-Colonial Identities in Africa*, London: Zed Books.

Tronvoll, K., 1998,– 'The Process of Nation-Building in Post-war Eritrea, Created from Below or Directed from Above?', *The Journal of Modern African Studies*, Vol. 36, No. 3, p. 461-482.

Conclusion

Donald P. Chimanikire

Democracy has always been at the heart of student demonstrations in African institutions of higher learning. The root cause of such demonstrations is found in the various University Acts themselves which envisage very undemocratic structures and administrations that are more suitable for civil departments or commercial companies than for academic institutions. For example, many African University Acts stipulate that the council shall be the governing body whereas the majority of council members are required to be non-academics. According to critics, such non-academics generally know nothing about how the university functions and only contribute in entrenching the managerial administrative system, which they are familiar with.

In many universities, vice-chancellors enjoy broad powers which allow them to: suspend any member of staff; prohibit the admission of a student or group of students to classes or to the university; expel or suspend any student or group of students; dissolve or suspend the students' union. Even many who believe that greater discipline is needed at the universities consider that many of the laws introduced by governments are disproportionately severe and will compromise the universities' generally good record of academic freedom and independence from governments.

Just as it is necessary to understand the character and development of higher education and further education, it is equally vital to know the circumstances under which African students live and study so as to understand the dynamics of students' movements or politics. This volume consists of accounts from four African countries: Cameroon, South Africa, Zimbabwe and Eritrea. The accounts focus on some very important aspects of the situation in which African students find themselves in many countries – a situation characterized by undemocratic university administrations, inadequate funding, poor living conditions and institutional and educational problems.

The four case studies from Africa clearly reveal that students' conditions in general have deteriorated since independence. The economic and political situation in the countries concerned has not made things easier. From the student's point of view, their economic, social and academic condition has been deteriorating at a steady pace since independence. Students are also gravely concerned about the cuts in educational funding. The cuts have affected students in all sorts of painful ways. The case studies highlight some of the sad realities. For example, the lack of essential learning materials, such as books and journals, and the very non-conducive learning environment, lack of adequate accommodation, sharing of rooms by several students, stinking toilets and leaking roofs are some of the students' grievances.

It is, therefore, not surprising that the most recent clashes between students and police were caused by students' demands for an increase in financial aid. African governments have been usually slow in responding to such demands and the financial aid given has been rejected by students as inadequate and disproportionate to the escalating living cost of living.

Moreover, the cuts, coupled with galloping inflation in some of the countries studied, have drastically curtailed students' purchasing power, not only with regard to food and lodging, but also books, stationary, and other practical training needs. In some cases, students show genuine concern for the plight of their teachers, most of whom are surviving by the skin of their intellect, frantically running around trying to get consultancies from international donors.

There are basically four issues which underlie the dramatic and often spectacular confrontation between students and the state that have come to dominate university politics in African universities, as highlighted by the case studies from Cameron, South Africa, Zimbabwe and Eritrea. Essentially, these hinge on efforts by African states to encroach on jealously guarded freedoms enjoyed by the universities. In recent years, African states have tried to appropriate the right to appoint top university officials. They have also adopted measures which impinge on academic freedom. They have attempted to stifle free speech on campuses. Moreover, they have ignored student welfare issues.

It should be recalled that, immediately after independence, university-state relations in Africa were, by and large, cordial. Disputes were resolved through dialogue. But this came to an end as African economies began to decline. The social composition of the various student bodies also changed following the opening up of education to all social groups after independence. Eventually the majority of the student population came from peasant and working class families. This meant they were more keenly aware of the consequences of the economic decline in the respective countries than their predecessors.

It is clear from the studies carried out in the four countries that in some of them economic decline also put an end to the 'anti-imperialist and anti-capitalist' alliance between the state and the students and other intellectual groupings in universities. Government policies were just not delivering the goods. Other subjective weaknesses, like corruption, nepotism and regionalism became prevalent. The failure of the African governments' political and economic policies led to the rise in frustration and militancy amongst students who increasingly began to feel the pinch.

For the student movements in higher educational institutions as revealed by cases in this volume, the grants issue has three essential elements: first, every student suffers in some way and is capable of being mobilized into action around demands for change; second, the level of grants is a crucial factor bearing on educational opportunity; third, inadequate grant levels will act as a disincentive to access to higher and further education -- a barrier particularly for working-class young people and those whose parents are unwilling or unable to provide a substantial subsidy.

Finally, it should be recognized that there has been a number of positive changes as a result of student pressure. The future will depend on the extent to which student movements and their allies are able to campaign effectively for reforms. Without the sternest opposition, many African governments' policies, as they are currently mapped out, will lead to a worsening of the situation in the years to come.

www.ingramcontent.com/pod-product-compliance
Lightning Source LLC
Chambersburg PA
CBHW070623300426
44113CB00010B/1636